otherwise grossly unremarkable

A MEMOIR OF CANCER

Ashleigh Matthews

BREAKWATER
P.O. Box 2188, St. John's, NL, Canada, A1C 6E6
www.breakwaterbooks.com

LIBRARY AND ARCHIVES CANADA CATALOGUING IN PUBLICATION

Title: Otherwise grossly unremarkable : a memoir of cancer / Ashleigh Matthews.

Names: Matthews, Ashleigh, author.

Identifiers: Canadiana 20240375599 | ISBN 9781778530265 (softcover)

Subjects: LCSH: Matthews, Ashleigh—Health. | LCSH: Cancer—Patients—Canada—Biography. | LCGFT: Autobiographies.

Classification: LCC RC265.6.M38 A3 2024 | DDC 362.19699/40092—dc23

We acknowledge the support of the Canada Council for the Arts. We acknowledge the financial support of the Government of Canada and the Government of Newfoundland and Labrador through the Department of Tourism, Culture, Industry and Innovation for our publishing activities.

PRINTED AND BOUND IN CANADA.

Canada Council for the Arts | Conseil des arts du Canada | Canada | Newfoundland Labrador

Breakwater Books is committed to choosing papers and materials for our books that help to protect our environment. To this end, this book is printed on a recycled paper that is certified by the Forest Stewardship Council®.

FSC www.fsc.org MIX Paper from responsible sources FSC® C103567

For Ava.

You teach me how to be authentic every day.

and for Bean.

You are the bravest person I've ever met.

I am so very proud of you both.

• • • • •

Truly, this book is dedicated to Scott.

Without your constant love and support
I'd never have found my strength to advocate,
to accept, to recover, to record, or to share.

I wrote it for them, but I dedicate it to you.

Once upon a time there was a cell.
The cell was within the duct of a breast,
and the breast was part of a body.
That body is mine, and that cell divided and divided
and invaded all the cells around it,
eventually becoming a carcinoma.

My name is Ashleigh,
and I'm a cancer survivor.

In 2019 I was diagnosed with breast cancer.

I am not unique in this experience, as the Canadian Cancer Society estimates that over 230,000 fellow Canadians were also diagnosed with some form of cancer during the same year that I was. I am, however, in a much smaller cohort of people diagnosed in young adulthood because I was thirty-five years old when I was diagnosed, thirty-four at the oldest when cancer began growing inside me. According to the Canadian Cancer Society, nine in ten people who are diagnosed with cancer are over the age of fifty.

Every one of those 230,000 cancer patients has a story, and there are likely aspects of each individual story that would resonate with any person diagnosed with this awful disease. There are also uniquely horrible challenges to be discovered among every demographic within the cancer community. I am speaking from the intersections of the cancer demographics that I represent: stage 3 breast cancer and a young-adult diagnosis. I never intend to minimize the struggles, fears, or challenges of any other type or stage of cancer when I share how awful my diagnosis and treatments were. Similarly, a cancer diagnosis is horrifying and frightening no matter what age the patient is, and I never intend to even suggest that receiving a cancer diagnosis under forty years of age is worse than any other age.

Among the most monumental challenges of being a young adult facing any kind of chronic and debilitating condition is that life keeps on going. Yes, it does for older adults and for kids too, but young adults face a plethora of unique circumstances in addition to the standard bullshit that comes with the diagnosis of a chronic illness. The fertility clock continues to tick for young adults who wish to be parents and are going through cancer treatment. Promotions, business growth opportunities, educational opportunities, they all carry on. That home down payment the young cancer patient had been saving for diligently for years can disappear in just a few months of pharmacy trips during active cancer treatment. For those starting their careers, their education and training, new relationships, for those at the beginning of significant life steps—and young adulthood promises a disproportionate amount—a cancer diagnosis is debilitating in ways that reach so much further than the years in which treatment happens. Few times, if at all, will opportunities for job advancement, educational enrichment, or the beginning of a new relationship truly wait for cancer to be felled.

Recognizing—feeling, really—the uniqueness of being so young but still an adult at the time of my diagnosis was an early and persistent isolating factor for me. I carry immense gratitude for those who shared their own deeply personal experiences of cancer with me early after my diagnosis. Their selfless giving of support and stories made me feel more prepared and less alone before every major step along the pathway of my cancer treatment. Their validation became my inspiration for sharing my own deeply personal experiences with those who will come through the hallways and hospital waiting rooms of oncology departments after me.

Speaking of inspiration, sometimes when I speak of the struggles of having cancer and facing mortality at a young age, I am told that I am inspirational purely because of what I have endured, or people will proclaim that they simply could not do what I have done. I firmly call bullshit on both of those assessments. Cancer is a horrid thing that happened to me, and I am strong for having chosen my route along this road. I am also strong for carrying through with that route when it got difficult. I am not inspirational for having survived it because what other choice did I have? Death—that was my alternative. Some people do choose that path after they've been exhausted and depleted by cancer to a depth they know they will never return from, and when the choice of death is deeply informed and consciously articulated by the patient who chooses it, then that's also pretty fucking strong.

Inspirational people can, however, be found in the research labs and among the scientists who push and push for better survival and efficacy rates for cancer treatments because they are the ones who have the choice to resign to defeat and stop pursuing their goals without balancing their own lives as the result of that resignation. In the vast majority of cases, if a cancer researcher decides to move on from a research project, there is no immediate or personally deadly side effect of that decision. Unlike my own decision to accept chemotherapy—the side effect of declining would have been my own death—a medical researcher who insists on continuing work to improve cancer treatments in the face of repeated failure is driven not by their own mortality but the mortality of those who are suffering. That's the shit that's inspirational to me.

One day, my two daughters will be old enough to comprehend what I went through as I battled cancer. One day, they will be able to read about cancer staging and grading and they will be able to grasp that it is only by a twist of cellular fate that I was placed on a road that did not divert me away from them. My oldest daughter might retain some memory of the time before her mom had cancer; however, my youngest daughter will grow up never holding a memory of a time before her mom lost her breasts. Throughout the treatments and medications I have endured, I have always been open and honest with my kids about what was happening using age-appropriate language. My children have seen me cry in frustration and anguish, have held my hand as I prepared to leave our home and go mourn the loss of a friend, and have watched me jump and scream for joy as I rang a bell commemorating the end of my active treatment phase. Throughout all of this, neither of my kids has ever asked if I was going to die because I have never given them the burden of understanding how close I came to that outcome. One day, though, they will be adults and they will figure that out. As my kids become adults, I wish for them to understand that I am here with them because of my own immense strength, which was unequivocally needed to endure treatments. I also wish for them to understand that those treatments were discovered, improved upon, and delivered to me by a multitude of medical researchers, doctors, and scientists over the course of careers they willingly returned to, day after day. I wish for them to know where inspiring people are truly found.

PART ONE

discovery / diagnosis

What we know is a drop,
what we don't know
is an ocean.

– SIR ISAAC NEWTON

CHAPTER ONE

—My breast feels weird, I texted my husband as we both lay in bed. Scott and I were bookending our kids as he read to them before bedtime, so while he was just an arm's length away from me, I could not speak my message aloud. My discovery was not one for our daughters' young ears to hear.

I found the mass one October evening as I reached across my youngest daughter, Bean, to point to an image on the page of the book we were enjoying. My older kid, Ava, was snuggled into her dad as I stretched my arm over towards the book in Scott's hands, and in doing so, I realized that the top of my right breast felt odd. There was no lump in the classic way I would have expected it to appear, just that the skin and the muscle above my nipple and up to my clavicle was hard. It was dense. It was alarmingly different. As Scott read a book to our children on the other side of the bed, I spiralled into a pit of anxiety.

I am a classic overthinker, which invariably devolves into worst-case-scenario thinking in situations like this. In fact, at the moment of discovery, I broke an Olympic record with the speed I gained moving from thinking *hmm, that's weird* to *well, I have breast cancer*. As an overthinker, it is impossible for me to find a mass in my breast and then calmly rationalize that there might be a dozen dull explanations for why it could be there before seeking diagnostic testing. Instead, I text my husband as I spiral into that anxiety pit and tell him that I found a mass, please call the coroner. Scott had known me for over fifteen years at this point and was no stranger to an overthinking wife, so once the kids were asleep he reminded me that all I could do was make an appointment with our general practitioner in the morning. This logical and action-oriented response was a mild balm to my racing brain, and it was also exactly what I did the next morning.

Less than a week after the discovery, I went to see my doctor regarding the denseness I'd found in my breast, despite the fact that he had performed a breast exam just a few months earlier as part of an annual check-up. During this appointment, he did a thorough exam, took notes, and told me to come back in two weeks when I would be at the opposite side of my ovulation and menstruation cycles. He wanted to take note of any changes that might happen to the mysterious denseness in relation to ovulation.

I had only just discovered this foreign invader and yet it immediately exerted a pull on my life. I charted the most mundane of its changes both emotionally via my constant awareness of its presence and literally with a pencil and paper over the course of the following two weeks. In early November, I arrived at my general practitioner's office, changed into the ubiquitous paper gown, sat on the segment of freshly unrolled disposable paper unfurled across the exam table, and waited to give him my report.

"Good day," he greeted me as he entered the examination room. "What brings you in today?"

"It's time for the two-week check-in. I'm here to update you on the changes in my breast."

"All right," he replied, pulling up my file on his computer and preparing to take notes. "Have you noticed any patterns in the changes you've experienced?"

I nodded. "The density . . . the heaviness, in my breast," I began, already reluctant to admit the obvious changes that were happening for fear of what it might indicate. "It's waxing and waning with my ovulation cycle. No doubt about that."

"Does it stay dense and just get denser?" he asked as he typed notes into my chart.

"No. It's almost as if it deflated slightly after my cycle began. It got heavier, harder, maybe? Just before ovulation and then, like a balloon with a hole poked in it, it deflated some after my cycle began." My hands mimicked a deflating balloon, as if this adult human wouldn't understand how a balloon behaves without hand signals.

"It's incredibly hard to explain," I consciously exhaled, "even though it's basically all I've focused on all week."

He gave me a wry smile. Having been my general practitioner for over a decade, he had also become well acquainted with my dual skill sets of overthinking and precise data collection.

"I think the change back and forth is less concerning than a constant growth. Cancer grows and continues to grow, so the waxing and waning, as you put it, is comforting . . ." He paused.

Here comes the downside.

"We still need to investigate further. Can you recall this type of change during any cycle before these last few months?" he queried.

"No," I answered immediately, but then I stopped to think deeper. "Actually, I don't know how accurately I can speak to that. I mean, I've been breastfeeding constantly for six years. My entire body has been all over the place for a long time, and Bean only stopped breastfeeding less than six months ago."

This connection hadn't occurred to me until the moment the words left my lips. Could this be an after-effect of the hormonal onslaught of pregnancy, breastfeeding, and parental exhaustion?

The hormonal traffic jam of breastfeeding was behind me now, so was this the new normal for my breasts?

My doctor read my mind with his response.

"You should remember that you're describing an enormous feat of milk production when measured by any yardstick. That productivity is all but guaranteed to affect your breast shape, size, overall feeling."

"This still doesn't seem . . . right," I pressed. "Why is there such a difference between my breasts? Only one breast is changing with my cycles. Why not both?"

"I agree. It's not average," he said, not looking at me as he made more notes about our conversation in my chart. "I'll request a routine ultrasound to rule out anything sinister, but you have curious symptoms worth investigating and nothing more."

I thanked him as he moved to exit the room. I redressed. I left the office with my faith set squarely on the power of diagnostic imaging as I exhaled for the first time since my arm grazed that mass a few weeks before.

CHAPTER TWO

It was a mild day for Newfoundland when I underwent my first breast ultrasound in December—six weeks after I had first spoken my concerns aloud to my general practitioner and less than two months since I'd found the heinous density. I went alone because the procedure was routine, and it was going to confirm what I so desperately wanted—no cancer here, silly!

After I'd changed into a gown, the ultrasound technician explained the procedure and told me that the radiologist would be in to perform the scan shortly. When the doctor came in, he waved the ultrasound wand over my gelled-up upper breast and within minutes declared me fine. He did not once move the wand below the nipple line of my right breast, nor did he scan at any angles around my nipple. I was still on the exam table when I was informed that I merely had dense tissue in my breast, something not uncommon for post-pregnancy breasts and even more common for breasts that had just recently finished breastfeeding. I was likely still levelling out on the hormone roller coaster that comes with no longer producing milk, and this denseness was just a side effect.

I left the examination room and returned to my belongings awaiting me in the high school gym class-style changing stalls just outside the ultrasound suite. I texted Scott to tell him that everything appeared to be fine as I pulled on my top layer of clothing, sending the message with an assurance I did not feel but had borrowed from the radiologist I'd briefly seen.

I arrived home to a hug from Scott, both of us relieved as the stress we had been carrying uncoiled. The drive home had given me ample opportunity to overthink the ultrasound experience from beginning to end, and I relayed that I felt that the entire ultrasound was over startlingly fast. I interpreted that as a sign that there was so little to see inside my body that the doctor didn't even have any spaces to pause over. I was so normal, I was boring. I viewed the brisk ultrasound as short and to the point due to its mundanity. I know now that I saw it that way because I so desperately needed science to tell the siren blaring inside me, warning me that something was wrong with my body, to shut up.

CHAPTER THREE

My kids have been homeschooled for their entire lives. In the weeks after my ultrasound, I was moving into the second semester of grade one with Ava, while Bean was three and a half. On an early January morning while getting dressed, I made a point to assess if the density of my breast had changed lately—something that had become routine following the lightning-fast ultrasound appointment the month before. This time, I immediately noted that my nipple also looked different.

Oooookay. What's going on here? I thought.

My nipple looked like it had been pressed down by something and hadn't quite come back into its normal place yet. This was curious because I had just showered and prior to that had been wearing a loose-fitting sports bra all night while sleeping. Neither of my breasts nor my nipple had been pressed on by anything with sufficient pressure to cause this amount of flattening.

I don't need this right now.

I forced myself to remain calm, to wait before panicking, by slowly adjusting my bra. Maybe if I gave my squashed nipple ample time to get itself back in line it would get its shit together and pop back out where it was supposed to be. It remained unmoved.

It stayed in that just-squashed position and, despite my silent pleas for normalcy, it didn't budge.

You have the images to prove that this isn't an issue.

I got dressed and started breakfast for everyone, plus ample amounts of coffee for myself.

Looking back, this might be my moment of deepest regret. I did not immediately listen to the siren that had been blaring in my subconscious since the moment I first detected a change in my body. Three months had passed since the first squawk of alarm, and seeing my nipple change so dramatically should have turned up the volume on that siren, and perhaps it did, but I didn't pay attention.

By the time I made a third appointment to talk to my general practitioner about my changing breasts, three more months had passed and my nipple had become so tucked under it looked almost inverted. By late April, I couldn't even coax it to come back to its former position if I physically pulled it out. Ultimately, it's possible that those three months did not make the difference between the road I travelled and a road that would have taken me over easier ground. However, when I added these three months of potential earlier diagnosis on top of the three months I already carried from the miss in my first diagnostic ultrasound, I had six months. Cancer can travel far in six months.

The second ultrasound I underwent happened in early May. I waited for my name to be called while sitting in the same waiting area as my first ultrasound, and then I changed out of my clothing and into a hospital gown in the same locker room stalls that I'd used the previous December.

The radiologist conducting my second breast ultrasound was not the same one who had carried out my first exam, and she began my appointment with the type of conversation a medical professional uses to help put a patient at ease when the appointment requires undressing.

"It's nice to finally see some warmer weather," she offered as I lay back on the examination bed.

"It certainly makes the walk from the car into the hospital easier," I replied with a smile.

"This will feel a little cold now," she explained as she squeezed the ultrasound gel onto the wand. She had the practiced ease of someone who has repeated this phrasing while carrying out this action countless times before. Next, she placed the wand on the top portion of the breast that had been at the root of my life hiccup for so many months.

"Huh," it was as much a sound as a word that she uttered.

There was no more friendly chatting about the weather or the temperature of the ultrasound gel now.

I looked to the technician assisting the radiologist for her reaction, hoping it would contradict my own assessment of the radiologist's change in demeanour upon seeing inside my body. Perhaps this is how she approached all of her diagnostic duties and I was once again overthinking a normal display of diligence from this doctor because, after all, we'd never met before this appointment. The technician's face, laser-focused on the radiologist, gave me no reason to relax. The radiologist's body language was telling both the technician and me that something specific and unexpected was pulling her attention, and it had begun as soon as she put the ultrasound wand to the dense portion of my right breast. The room shrunk and all that existed in the world was this radiologist and the screen she remained hyper-focused on.

There was near silence in the room as she examined the dense breast tissue from every conceivable angle. Next, she went over and around my now fully inverted nipple and through every conceivable angle, and over all the flesh of my breast under my nipple as well.

"I don't like the density of this breast at all," she finally revealed.

Samezies, I think but am unable to force the quip past my lips.

"I want you in a mammogram machine for sharper images on these dense areas. It will also help us understand what's going on behind your nipple."

Did she say areas? As in, more than one?

"I'm referring you for a mammogram immediately," she concluded with authority.

Gut punch.

Breathe.

"What's the timeline like for getting in for a mammogram?" I asked. Quiet voice and dry mouth.

"I'm calling right now," she replied as she turned from me to the telephone on the desk next to the ultrasound monitor and dialled a four-digit internal hospital number. Evidently "immediately" meant just that: *immediately*. Not simply the referral—the mammogram itself. I looked to the ultrasound technician on my other side as she put a hand on my arm and offered a strong smile.

I was simultaneously cold and sweating. I covered my chest with the flimsy cotton sides of the hospital gown. I didn't know where to put my hands or what to look at as the call between the radiologist and her colleague continued.

Should I ask for my clothing? Do I change out of this hospital gown, or is the mammogram happening in the same room, somehow?

I was unable to comprehend the logistics of moving from one examination space to another when the movement was driven by such medical urgency that this next test could happen literally immediately.

After a quiet and quick conversation, the phone was laid back in the cradle.

"She just finished up with the last appointment," the radiologist told me. "The timing is perfect. She's waiting for you now."

Who is waiting for me? Where are they waiting?

Questions that I, once again, could not put together into

phonograms and phrases to ask this doctor who had just arranged a mammogram for me with lightning speed.

"It's okay," the radiologist replied to my immobile silence, "let's go. I'll walk you to the mammogram room." As she said this, she was already pulling my boots out from underneath the end of the ultrasound bed. She radiated patience as she waited for me to pull them on and then add a second hospital gown in reverse to cover my chest. As promised, the radiologist personally walked me down several corridors and into the room where the mammography technician was waiting for us.

The contrast between this experience—the response of this medical professional after seeing a diagnostic image of my breast versus the previous ultrasound that I had experienced—was more jarring than the mammogram itself. Add in the rapid transition from ultrasound suite to mammogram machine and I barely had time to process the pancaking of my breasts between the mammography plates.

While my body was in the mammogram machine, my mind, my emotions, my spirit, were focused on the forced neutrality of the radiologist's face when she saw the inside of the density on the ultrasound screen. A highly educated professional in the fields of both cancer and diagnostic imaging had seen something occurring inside my breast that she did not like, and she was not going to allow me to leave without more investigation.

"Could you place your arm up here and hold this handle, love," asked the mammography technician, jolting my mind back into the environment occupied by my body. Hospital gown open, one breast squashed in a metal mammogram machine the height and colour of a tarnished C3PO.

"How quickly will these images be back?" I asked as she further adjusted my positioning with a gentle twist of my shoulders.

"It won't take long, dear, a few days at most for them to be reviewed. I expect it'll feel like an eternity for you, though."

She stepped behind the protective radiation screen to capture more photos of the denseness, and I wondered if anyone had ever spoken truer words to me in my life.

CHAPTER FOUR

Three days after my combination ultrasound-mammogram, my general practitioner called me to tell me that a mass had been found lurking behind my right nipple. The composition of the mass was not evident from the mammogram imaging alone, and thus it necessitated a core biopsy—a significantly more invasive diagnostic test than anything I had experienced up to this point.

Words like *benign* and *malignant* surfaced in my head.

Movie scenes where people hold hands with their loved ones and are told by stoic doctors in white lab coats that "it's cancer" were my only touchstones for news like this, but no one watches those scenes for direct advice on how to react when it's happening to you.

I couldn't claim I was exactly surprised. I'd known something was happening to that breast, behind that nipple, for months. Further, I had suspected it was something sinister for weeks. I had begun *really* listening to that siren blaring inside me ever since I experienced the diligent look of focus on the radiologist's face during the ultrasound just days before. There is a difference between not feeling surprised at hearing a doctor tell you they'd found a mass inside your body and truly believing that the mass existed at that second. A mass with unknown abilities.

The next day, the booking department called to schedule a biopsy appointment in the early afternoon for just two days later.

"I thought wait times for medical testing were maddeningly long in St. John's," Scott replied when I told him that I would be undergoing a biopsy only six days after I'd had the mammogram that confirmed there was a mass in my breast. Speed has a way of turning a health question mark into an exclamation point, and we both felt the urgency in the extremely short timeline between appointments, although our mirrored fear went unspoken at that moment.

"They are. This is bad, Scott."

"You don't know that yet," he firmly replied.

"It's not good," I shot back, and I could tell he didn't have the strength to pretend to disagree.

"What's this next test, the biopsy? Is it surgery?"

"No," I said, yet I faltered at this thought. "At least, I don't think so."

Is *this surgery*?

"It's called a 'core biopsy' and they're doing it via mammogram since that's the test that found the mass. I guess there could be an ultrasound biopsy if that's how they identified it?" I concluded without conviction.

"Core as in centre. So, they're taking a sample from the centre of the mass, then," he reasoned.

"It sounds intense for sure. I can't lift anything heavy for a week afterwards, and I may leave with two or three stitches," I replied. Resigned to whatever this test involved, I reached for my favourite coping mechanism, the dark joke. "I might have a bitchin' scar, though!"

The core biopsy procedure was carried out in the same department as the mammogram imaging I had undergone the week before, which meant I was back in the same waiting room I had been in twice already, but this time with Scott. I chose to stand along the wall and pace slowly behind the plastic chairs in the waiting room with the hope of siphoning off some of my anxiety.

Scott attempted to counter the worry causing my relentless pacing across the hallway tiles.

"Think of it like this: this may be the last time you have to wait outside an exam room and worry that you have—"

"Don't say it," I cut him off as I paced in front of him. "Don't say the name of the thing I may have."

"Fear of a name increases fear of the thing itself. Isn't that the quote? Don't 'Voldemort' this situation when you don't even know whether it is or isn't," he replied.

"You didn't say the word either, Dumbledore."

"Ashleigh Matthews," called a nurse in light-blue scrubs.

Scott kissed me on the cheek and I followed Blue Nurse down a short corridor.

We entered an exam room containing a small desk, several chairs, and a mammogram machine, and the nurse gave me a hospital gown to change into. Another nurse, this one in teal scrubs, came into the room as I slipped behind the retractable curtain in the corner to change out of my sweater and shirt. Once I returned with my new threads on, Teal Nurse greeted me warmly before beginning to explain the procedure to me.

"You had a mammogram recently," she began, "so we'll get you set up and take images just the same as you had done last time." She then indicated a computer screen and equipment controls just to the side of the mammogram machine, behind which Blue Nurse was standing.

"The images are immediately visible on this screen," Teal Nurse explained. "Once we have taken an initial set of images, the pathologist will come in and begin the biopsy. It can sound and look frightening, so I want you to be prepared for the tools that will be used. The core extractor sounds like the noise made by a dentist drill, and you will feel a vibration from its movement."

"All right," my reply came out automatic and dull, as if I was being given the weather forecast and not being told what to expect as a dentist drill probed into one of my most sensitive body parts. Shock in the moment deadened my reflexes and responses.

"We'll freeze the area well before the biopsy starts, of course, but you will likely feel pressure as the core is being sampled," she continued calmly.

"Okay," I nodded weakly in reply. Intense mental weight pressed on me, born of the fact that a procedure this invasive and involved was warranted. I was pinned to that chair by fear as I listened to her descriptions. These were the things that would be happening to me just minutes after she spoke the sentences.

"It's crucial that you try to remain as still as you can, Ashleigh," Blue Nurse stressed, stepping out from behind the monitor. "Once the core is biopsied, the doctor will take the sample directly to a microscope in another room in order to confirm that the sample is from the exact mass that was identified on the images taken."

"Does that mean there will be answers right away? Do I wait out with my husband?"

"Ashleigh, you will be staying as still as you can in that chair. Your breast will stay under the plates of the mammogram machine while the pathologist looks at your tissue samples under the microscope," explained Teal Nurse. "We need to ensure that the mass that was identified on the imaging is included in the material extracted in the biopsy. We can only do that if we compare the sample right away. We need you to stay still in the same position you were in when the images were taken in case the mass needs to be resampled. You don't want to go through all of this only to find out that the biopsy missed the mass. You'd have to come back and do it all again," Blue Nurse explained. The rationalization that I only wanted to be here once rang loud and true.

"How long does it take?" I asked, resigned to both the absurdity and also the necessity of how this before/after biopsy comparison would be carried out.

"I promise you, the pathologist will be swift," assured Blue Nurse.

The biopsy took half an hour or so in real time; however, it felt significantly longer to me as I was topless and pinched by one breast in an oversized drill press, unable to move. I left the breast-screening clinic of the hospital accompanied by Scott and with a teeny ice pack pressed on my swollen right breast. I had not needed stitches, but the biopsy site was sore already and had required several thin bandages to close the wound in my skin. I lamented the fact that the biopsy site was going to leave that bitchin' scar after all.

Scott and I went home and we finished preparing for a party we were throwing at our house the next day to celebrate our kids' birthdays. Ava and Bean were turning four and seven that weekend regardless of whether I had an ice pack and bandage on my breast or not, so we gathered with friends as planned to eat pizza and blow bubbles into the spring air.

In less than a week I would be told that I did, indeed, have cancer.

CHAPTER FIVE

The phone call came early on Friday morning, six days after the dual birthday party. I had anticipated that it would take two weeks to hear back regarding the pathology of my core biopsy, and while I had been thinking about my tissue samples threading their way through the microscopes of a series of professionals within the medical system all week, I did not believe anyone would find cancer cells. I thought about it in the same way I think about winning the lottery: wondering what I would say, do, feel in the moment of receiving the news but never believing it would actually occur.

When the phone rang, I was helping Ava collect her things for an afternoon with her friends at forest school. The ringing of my phone on that morning was the auditory manifestation of the siren that had been blaring inside my subconscious, emanating from inside the cells of my breast, since the previous October. It was the siren telling me something was deathly wrong, coming to life in the form of the chime on my phone and then the voice of a known and beloved receptionist from the office of my general practitioner.

"Hello?" I answered, half distracted by my ongoing discussion with Ava about hummus versus carrot sticks for the final addition to her lunch bag.

"Ashleigh, it's the clinic," the office receptionist said. "The doctor wants you to come in immediately."

"Oh. Okay, that was faster than anticipated. Finally, I can put this behind me," I said in a fumbling attempt to ascertain the direction of the report from the phone call.

"I can be in whenever you can fit me next week. Monday? Tuesday morning is tight . . ." I trailed off, already envisioning the appointment in my mind. We would look over the pathology of something that needed addressing, like an abscess or a cyst of some kind. Something that could not be dismissed but was not fatal; something that would give me a story to attach to that small dimple of scar I was going to carry from the biopsy site.

"No, honey. Today," she replied with kindness. "You're on the schedule for one o'clock today." She repeated the word "today" with the same kindness but also the added authority of a medical professional conveying to me that I would not be missing this appointment. "Bring Scott with you when you come in and, Ashleigh, if you can leave the kids with a friend or family, you should do that, too."

My vision narrowed. My mouth went totally dry, then my tongue stopped responding to brain commands. I managed to look towards a clock and see that it was just past ten o'clock in the morning and quickly calculated that Scott was likely about to take his morning break.

"Okay," I replied in a whisper. "I can do that."

"Ashleigh. You'll be with Scott, right? He's coming too?" she reiterated. I registered that she was repeating my name often, drawing my attention to the point upon which her directions were placed.

I'm dying.

I knew this because no one insists that someone bring their spouse to the doctor to find out nothing is wrong. She wouldn't have me drop the kids and bring my husband for the doctor to tell me I have post-breastfeeding breast density. Over the phone, I heard the clicking of a keyboard being used by another person in the vicinity of the receptionist and I remembered that she had asked me a question.

"Yes." I am robotic. "With Scott, no kids," I repeated her instruction. "One o'clock."

"See you both then."

The phone was heavy in my hand and I was dizzy and hot. I didn't remember what I had been doing before it rang, and I didn't know how to move myself through time and space from that moment in which the bomb detonated to the next moment where I would receive a report on the damages of that explosion. My life had been cleaved into two eras—the Before Cancer era had just ended and now, suddenly, it was the beginning of the After Cancer era.

"Hey. What's up?'" Scott said cheerfully as he picked up the phone. I was calling from within this new era and his voice was far away and muffled. I had called him to sever his life and begin the new timeline for him, too. I had to slice his world just as it had been done to mine minutes ago if he was to come with me.

"They called," I whispered, "I am to be in the office at one o'clock." My voice began to disappear as I travelled farther down the lines of instruction given by the receptionist. "With you. She specifically said to bring you."

"What?" The volume of his voice increased by the same factor that mine had lowered. He heard me, but he had not understood what I was saying.

"She said to bring you. She said not to bring the kids," I relayed. "Scott, I'm scared."

"I'm leaving right now. I'm literally walking out the side door right now," he reported to me.

"Scott. I have cancer."

I said it.

"You do not know that," his voice weak, fearful. I heard a steel door slam shut and I could tell that he was walking outside now. In my mind, I see the parking lot and can imagine him briskly walking to our vehicle.

Did he even get his jacket?

"She didn't tell me to bring you because she misses seeing your face," I said as I heard the beep-beep of the car doors unlocking, the engine starting. Then we hung up.

I placed my phone on top of the dresser and lay on the bed in my bedroom, certain that I was going to die. Ava was in her bedroom across the hall debating sweater choices for her afternoon outside, while Bean and all her stuffies kept Ava company.

They're too young for this.

I'm *too young for this.*

There were too many minutes between that moment and the three hours that had to pass before I received my death sentence, and from the deepest parts within my very essence I simply did not know what to do. These are the minutes that constitute the only time during my battle with cancer that I fully and completely gave up. I was twisting in the gravity at the very beginning of an entirely new era of time in my life, one that came upon me with the speed and force of an atomic blast. Within these first few precarious moments at the beginning of this After Cancer era, I had nothing within me to summon to fight cancer. I had nothing within me at all because I actually had cancer cells within me, and I wasn't supposed to have cancer to begin with. After my world was split into two, I pre-gave up on moving forward in the new era.

I lay on the bed, two walls and one universe away from my young children, and I stayed there unmoving for twenty minutes. Then the genesis of the gravity in my life, Scott, arrived home. He told me we needed to figure out what the ever-loving-fuck was going on first and then we'd take it one step at a time. I was no longer alone in this new era. We have a saying in our house whenever a person is facing a seemingly impossible task—which, admittedly, was never even close to the task of fighting cancer—one person would say, "How do you eat an elephant?" and the other person would reply, "One bite at a time." Scott reminded me just by laying on the bed beside me while we waited to go see the doctor, knowing so fully that it was bad news, that not only was I going to have to take this one bite at a time, but that whenever I dropped my fork, he would always be there to hand it back to me.

The hours between the phone call and the appointment passed in a time warp that felt like seconds and an eternity. Memories like snapshots are all that remain: snacks and sweaters chosen; kids secured in car seats; Ava dropped at her forest school; Bean dropped at the home of a dear friend that lived close by.

Three hours after the phone had rung, Scott and I arrived at the doctor's office. Once again, I found myself sitting silently in a waiting room, an action I'd repeated more in the past month than in all the time since giving birth to Bean. There was no one else there to share the space with us, a fact I suspect was less coincidence and more a kind intention on the part of the clinic staff. It didn't take long for me to be called in, and I stood up to move to the exam room and simultaneously inch closer to the confirmation of my imminent demise, with my husband steadfastly behind me. My doctor walked in the room and closed the door and, in my six years of being his patient, he'd never looked so pale.

I was mid-stride in pacing the length of the exam room, another attempt to siphon off some of my anxiety, when he greeted us both and I immediately cut him off.

"Just say it," I demanded. "It's cancer."

He nodded. "Yes."

I sank to the floor and wailed. I don't remember what Scott or my doctor said in those first few minutes after receiving confirmation that I did have cancer. I don't remember how long I sat on the floor and cried. These parts of my memories are lost to the bulldozer that is grief, to the bulldozer that is cancer. I do know that neither of the men sharing the exam room with me hurried my pain along or shied away from it in any visible way.

Eventually, I realized I had moved across the room and was sitting on the floor beside Scott's chair. I had my head in his lap, tears soaking into the leg of his jeans. It was impossible to tell which eyes they had come from as we both contributed to this liquid collection of pain. Scott's hand on my back was trembling, and it shattered my heart to feel the manifestation of pain that my cancer was already heaping upon him.

My doctor continued filling in the specifics of the findings of my biopsy. He never once rushed me to listen to him, never once rushed me to stop crying, never once displayed impatience when asked a question he'd already answered.

"What the biopsy found is called ductal carcinoma in situ," he said. "It means that it is a cancer that is contained fully within the duct of the breast and cannot move. That's what 'in situ' means, actually. Latin for 'in place,'" he added reassuringly—definitions and trivia offered to lower the ratio of silence to pain in the room.

"Do I have to do chemotherapy?" I asked. It was my first direct question since he nodded his head to confirm that cancer was residing within my body.

"No, no. An extremely early cancer detection like this means that it hasn't even had time to move. It hasn't had time to go anywhere, even if it could, so there would be no need for anything as extreme as chemotherapy. That is for later-stage cancers. I think this ductal cancer—it's also called DCIS—might even be a stage 0."

"Whatever stage it is, the fucker is being removed from my body," I declared. "The other breast, too."

"You'll have lots of time to make decisions like that, but you will likely only need a lumpectomy on that side and nothing more," he cautioned immediately. "When breast cancer is present, this is the best-case scenario in terms of the timing of discovery. I don't suggest celebration—it's going to be a rough few months with surgery and scans, but it's going to be behind you before you know it," he concluded.

"The ductal stuff—," I began.

"Ductal carcinoma," he helped, "but just remember 'DCIS.'"

"DCIS. That's why my nipple started pulling in?" I queried.

"I am certainly not an oncologist. Explaining the exact mechanisms of your cancer is above my pay grade, and you will have time to ask an oncologist or a surgeon specific questions soon," he prefaced. "But yes, this is what was found right behind your nipple. It might also be why the areas above and at the top of the breast are dense. Your body is responding to the foreign cell behaviour and perhaps even attempting to isolate it," he offered.

"Why was it changing with my ovulation cycles?" I asked him, questions forming as my emotional onslaught slowed and my brain began to reconnect to my body.

"Honestly, I don't have an answer for that. I wondered that myself when I received this report, but any finding is a direction to start with, and it sets out a treatment path that will hopefully give that question an answer as well."

The honesty my doctor showed by telling me that he did not know the answer to my question illuminated the fact that this news was not crashing into Scott and me alone. My doctor's tone was one of shock; he was stunned at the finding and he was experiencing a version of this diagnostic riptide along with me. He had not simply received this news and passed it on, his participation in the severing of my life into the After Cancer era had taken a toll on his own emotions as well.

"Well, record this in my chart: I am having a bilateral mastectomy and not a lumpectomy to address this. I will never relive this day and these weeks again for as long as I live."

Scott and I left the office and we sat in our car in the parking lot and cried. We drove home and cried some more and began the process of adjusting our reality to include cancer.

CHAPTER SIX

During the appointment when my general practitioner levelled me with the reality of having cancer, he'd also told me that the pathology report suggested requesting yet another ultrasound of what was no longer simply my "breast denseness," but now my ductal carcinoma. The report also specified the inclusion of an ultrasound of the lymph nodes located in my armpit on my right side. I now understand that this request is not a standard diagnostic step for a person with ductal carcinoma in situ, so perhaps one of the pathologists who viewed my samples had a sense that something more was at work.

The third radiologist I interacted with in the breast ultrasound suite was equally as wonderful as the previous radiologist who had rushed me to get a mammogram, and this radiologist almost managed to conceal the flash of concern that crossed her face the moment the wand touched my right armpit. She hid it so well, I almost didn't catch it.

"What diagnosis have you received already, Ashleigh?" she asked as she searched the screen in front of her for signs of health or disease.

"DCIS. I gather that is why my nipple is hiding all the time,"

I gestured to the nipple on my exposed right breast that was maintaining its exceptional turtle impression and was fully pushed into the flesh of my breast. "That breast is not long for this body. They'll both be gone before this entire ordeal is behind me."

"I often think I would make that same choice if I was in your shoes," she broke focus on the screen to make eye contact with me and smile as she said this. "Do you know if you have been referred to a surgeon yet?"

"Yes. My first appointment is next week, actually," I replied.

Our conversation carried on casually as she continued to view the blurry black and white images of the inside of my body on her screen, but I did not miss the pointed looks exchanged with the ultrasound technician sitting on my other side. I also did not fail to notice when the radiologist reached for a tray of instruments set behind the monitor.

"The lymph nodes in your collarbone look great. They're exactly what I would expect to see," she began to explain. "However, a few under your right armpit—the axillary lymph nodes—are swollen," she concluded.

I did not understand many of these words or understand how fearful I should have been upon hearing them; however, I was basically at peak fear already, so there was nowhere higher for me to go—or so I thought.

"The best move now would be to do an immediate needle aspiration. I'll extract some of the fluid from inside a plump node so that it can be checked for cancer cell activity." She maintained eye contact as she spoke to me and then rested a hand on my arm. "A needle biopsy today will provide the fastest answer to why those lymph nodes are swollen."

I would have done just about anything to have a complete and accurate answer to the question of what was going on within my body, so I agreed before she even completed her argument for why

I should get it done right away.

"I want to figure all this out as soon as possible," I said, nodding in agreement with her suggested course of action. "A needle biopsy right now is fine as long as someone will hold my hand, please."

The ultrasound technician held my hand while the radiologist extracted yet another small piece of me destined for the microscope of a pathologist.

Despite dipping my toe in the waters of cancer, I was still very much a novice to its terms, tricks, and timelines at this point. I would come to learn that in the circles of young adults who have cancer, those on the outside—those people who have not themselves had cancer nor handed the fork to a beloved person who does—are referred to as Cancer Muggles. In the Harry Potter series, a muggle is a non-magical person. It is someone who does not know what it's like to have magical ability; therefore, a Cancer Muggle is someone who does not know what it's like to live through, and live with, cancer.

I was still firmly a Cancer Muggle on the day I experienced an unexpected needle biopsy of my right axillary lymph nodes. I knew I had cancer, yet because I had been told that I had stage 0 DCIS that had been caught early, I felt like I had Cancer Lite. I'd assumed I was attending this ultrasound only as a matter of routine diagnostics after already finding evidence of a stage 0 cancer in my ducts; that it was simply a quick stop on the pathway before surgery. I wasn't going to have to undergo any of the horrible culturally stereotypical aspects of cancer—losing my hair, throwing up, dying—because I'd just have one surgery and get on with it. I had checked out some books on cancer from the library, but because they contained so much information that didn't feel applicable to my understanding of the cancer I had, I hadn't read much within them. This early omission of research on my behalf was a fortuitous thing, as I did not understand the magnitude of a plump lymph node as I lay on that exam table holding the hand of a stranger while a thin needle carefully investigated inside my body for yet another cancer bomb.

Just days after the third ultrasound, I received another call from the receptionist of my general practitioner's office asking for me to come in. Asking me to bring support. Asking me to leave the kids home. Again, I knew I must have cancer in my lymph nodes. I suspected that this finding would change the course of my treatment; however, this time, I did not lie on the bed and give up. I know now that this difference was mostly due to the ignorance that being a Cancer Muggle gave me. While I understood that cancer being present in another place in my body was not great, I still did not yet understand how royally shitty it truly was.

CHAPTER SEVEN

Once again, speed added an exclamation mark to my cancer, making it seem more like *Cancer!!!* Three days after my general practitioner informed me of the cancer cells found in my lymph nodes, I had my first meeting with another physician, my oncology surgeon, at the Cancer Centre in St. John's. The largest adult general hospital in Newfoundland and Labrador—the Health Sciences Centre—and the Cancer Centre are contained within the same expanse of buildings that also includes a variety of other medical and laboratory facilities. Most of the buildings are connected to each other, and all the buildings share the same collection of oddly shaped and inconveniently placed public parking lots. This meeting with my oncology surgeon was my first time attending an appointment inside the Cancer Centre, but because it was located within the same footprint as the general hospital, it was not a wholly unfamiliar location for either Scott or me. On this day, we parked in a lot we'd utilized many times over the years for prenatal and post-natal appointments, various specialist appointments, and when visiting hospitalized friends and family.

"How're you feeling now that we're here?" Scott asked as we walked across the parking lot. It was a beautiful mid-June day and there was no speed in our step as we made our way from the outdoor sunshine towards the recirculated air and fluorescent lighting of the hospital.

"I feel..." I paused, assessing. "Relieved to finally be taking a step towards removing the cancer," I replied. "Maybe surgery can happen quickly enough that we won't miss the entire camping season."

"Maybe. The first priority is getting this cancer out of you, but I have no doubt you can move through that quickly and get back on your feet," Scott replied.

"I still feel insistent that I'm having both of my breasts removed. I am absolutely having a mastectomy and not a lumpectomy and I am having both breasts removed," I stated with conviction. "The appointments, the biopsies," I paused again, mentally flipping through the calendar of days since my second ultrasound, "these past few weeks have taken more years off my life than the fucking cancer has and I can't even think about having to do this again."

"I think I would make the same choice," he quietly agreed, just as he reached out to hold open the large glass door leading to the front lobby of the Cancer Centre, and I passed through for the first time as a patient.

Once registered, we sat in the waiting area for Clinic A. In what felt like no time at all, a nurse called my name and we followed her back into the labyrinth of examination rooms. She gave me a gown to change into, recorded my height and weight, and told us both that it wouldn't be a long wait for the oncology surgeon to arrive in the room.

Maybe if I had read more about lymph nodes in those library books that were still sitting on my bedside table I would have been better prepared for the crackling reality of advanced cancer that was about to descend onto my world. Maybe I wouldn't have sat on the exam table in a drafty hospital gown chatting with my husband about how easy or difficult it may be for him to take time off work in a few weeks for my surgery. Our assumptions that I would leave that room with a surgery timeline set for the very near future were deeply set, and those assumptions were built by the Cancer Muggles that we were, even as we both had the knowledge that the cancer was not confined to my breast ducts.

"Hi Ashleigh," greeted the surgeon as he stepped inside the examination room. "How are you doing today?" He then turned from me to greet and introduce himself to Scott as well. Immediately behind him was the nurse that had shown me into the examination room. She followed him into the room and closed the door behind her.

"Well, I am topless and in the Cancer Centre. It's not a gold-star day for me," I replied.

"Fair," he countered. "Few people are happy to meet me under these circumstances." He paused here and allowed the atmosphere in the room to change from one of a cordial greeting between strangers to a professional discussion regarding the serious issue at hand.

"You already know that I'm an oncology surgeon. I will be involved in whatever surgery option we decide is best for your care," he explained, then paused again to invite the nurse sitting at his side to introduce herself and her role during the appointment.

"I'm here to take some notes for you so you don't need to focus on recording what is discussed," she explained, producing a pen and notepad. "This way, you can both be present in the conversation and you'll have these notes to review if you need to later."

"Ashleigh, tell me what you understand of your diagnosis today," the surgeon asked me while looking down at the chart he was holding. As he flipped it open, I could see my name printed on the outer front edge. The chart carried a sizable heft considering that this was my first appearance at the Cancer Centre as a patient.

"I have cancer in my breast. A ductal carcinoma that is behind my right nipple and is causing it to pull under," I began. "There were signs of cancer found under my right arm as well, so that's not great," I concluded while indicating to my right armpit with a wave of my left hand.

"You've received the report on the lymph nodes already, then?" he asked, looking up from the chart and towards me sitting on the examination table. His tone conveyed surprise at the news that I was aware of the newest pathology report.

"My general practitioner told us this past Friday," I relayed, looking to Scott for confirmation as he nodded at me. "I heard about the cancer discovery for the first time two weeks ago, and then the lymph nodes three days ago. Honestly, I just want to know when I am going to have surgery and get the cancer out of my body," I explained. I felt desperate for the feeling of control given when action is being taken to address a problem.

"I understand that you are anxious to move towards surgery. It is going to be a key part of your treatment plan, but Ashleigh, do you understand what the findings in your lymph nodes indicate for the larger picture of your cancer?" he pressed gently.

Why didn't I look up "lymph nodes" in those library books I had all weekend?

I felt a flush of regret, a flush of panic. The examination room felt like it was collapsing around me and it was all I could do not to be crushed by the walls and ceiling as they tipped inward and descended towards me.

"I . . . well, I guess no," I haltingly began. "Based mostly on how this conversation is going right now, I don't think I understand how that factors in at all," I hurriedly admitted.

"It means that your treatment plan will not be determined by a finding of DCIS," he informed me. "Rather, it means that it will be guided by a finding of DCIS and also something else along with the DCIS. There is another type of cancer in your body that has travelled to the lymph nodes and shed the cancer cells found there by the needle biopsy," he explained.

"Wait," Scott sat straight upright and asked with panic, "where is the other cancer? Is there cancer in two places?"

"Right now we know there is DCIS in the right breast and we know there are cancer cells in the right axillary lymph nodes," he explained as he turned to address Scott directly. "We know that those axillary cancer cells did not originate from the DCIS because ductal carcinoma does not travel. There has to be another carcinoma somewhere in the breast that does have the ability to metastasize—or move—outside of the breast," he reasoned, turning back to me now to ensure I was also following the explanation he was giving us. "That cancer is what has been deposited in the lymph nodes."

"Holy shit," Scott whispered, sitting back in his chair.

"Fuck," I added, curling into myself on the exam table.

"Exactly," confirmed the surgeon.

"How did this get missed?" Scott asked forcefully to the room and not directly to the surgeon. "She had an ultrasound last year that found nothing. If cancer was there then, how was it not detected?" Scott was arguing with the diagnosis itself, negotiating with reality as it faced him. An anger was born in my husband at that moment, the product of the seeds planted by the mistakes made during my first ultrasound. As he was seeing only how the past could have prevented this present, at that moment I was seeing only the future that must unfurl in order for me to continue having a present at all.

"What do I do now?" I said. In spite of sweating palms, flushed face, and a dry mouth, I connected these words. I felt blindsided, yet the finding of cancer in my lymph nodes was known to me all weekend, and I had not grasped what it meant. I felt embarrassed at my lack of understanding, embarrassed that the feeling of being blindsided in this moment was the fault of my own inaction in researching the new cancer finding. Above all, I felt embarrassed at my confidence just an hour ago while walking into this appointment, so sure I would leave with a surgery plan.

"The path forward will be decided with your medical oncologist. You're young, so there will be several options to consider. Surgery will be one aspect of your treatment plan, and I will be here to talk through those surgical options with you when the time comes, but that is not the first step you will likely take," he reported.

"What's first?" I barely whispered, drowning in the fear of the realization I'd already made. Suffocating under the weight of the real question I was asking without speaking the word inside my head.

"If you wish to fully eradicate the cancer that has presented in your breast and also your lymph nodes, chemotherapy should be the first part of your treatment plan."

"Chemotherapy," I repeated, yet I scarcely made a sound. I mouthed the word.

"Why didn't the biopsy find both kinds of cancer?" Scott asked, as quietly as I had ever heard him speak. His anger replaced by the same suffocating realization, the same embarrassment at his own ignorance from just an hour ago.

The surgeon turned to him and answered with the same patient, calm tone and understanding he had shown throughout the appointment.

"The biopsy aimed to take a sample from the mass that was identified on the mammogram, and it was successful in doing that. The mammogram imaging identified a mass behind the right nipple, and the biopsy found DCIS in that mass," he recapped. "We only know that there must be an additional carcinoma somewhere else in the breast because of the evidence in the lymph nodes," he reasoned. "It's as if we have discovered the footprints of invasive cancer before seeing the tumour itself. It's a diagnosis that has been made in reverse order from the usual pattern."

"Chemotherapy is . . . extreme," I said. I was so slow to move, so slow to process, that I had remained behind in the conversation, stuck in the tar that was the news of chemotherapy. "So I have cancer that necessitates chemotherapy?" I questioned. "I thought I had stage 0 cancer?" It was my turn to negotiate with reality as it faced me.

"Yes, DCIS is sometimes considered 'stage 0,'" the surgeon replied, switching from the conversation with Scott about diagnostic efficacy and back to the conversation with me about chemotherapy. "Ashleigh, you no longer have just that type of cancer. We can't tell exactly what stage cancer you do have until the additional tumour is found, but you are not a stage 0 cancer patient anymore. We know you have invasive cancer somewhere in your breast because your cancer has spread at least as far as your lymph nodes. In order to increase the likelihood of removing every cell of that cancer from your body, you need to view chemotherapy as a foundational aspect of your treatment," he said, maintaining eye contact.

The nurse behind him continued scribbling non-stop on her notepad, recording every pertinent aspect of this new reality of mine. I remained stuck so far down in tar that I couldn't believe the volume of words that she was recording had been spoken.

"I can choose not to," I stated.

"You won't, though," Scott immediately said, looking directly at me.

"You could," the surgeon conceded.

"What would you want your wife to do if she were in these shoes?" Scott asked.

"I would 100 per cent want her to accept chemotherapy," he shared with no hesitation.

"Fuck these shoes," I added.

"Yep," agreed the nurse. "Young patients come in here and face this treatment plan and it is hard, but they do it and just crush it. You can do that too," she stated with a confidence I did not share.

"We have two kids. Two girls," Scott said, as much to himself as to anyone in the room.

"Then you need to be here for them," the nurse responded, looking at me. She then moved to sit beside me on the examination table.

I cannot begin to understand the emotional burden the doctors and nurses who work within the Cancer Centre carry when they have to explain to otherwise healthy adults that they are, in fact, going to die without immediate and significant invasive intervention. If this surgeon or nurse felt anything akin to frustration or emotional exhaustion while they sat with me and told me in no uncertain terms that I would need to choose to do chemotherapy, to lose my hair, to have surgery, if I wanted to fully and wholly eradicate my cancer they did not show me an iota of those feelings.

The nurse, still sitting beside me, continued to take notes for me on the pad of paper. Despite the trauma of these moments, I focused on her handwriting curling across the page and forming the heading "Lymphatic System".

"The lymphatic system is a superhighway, and the cancer in your breast jumped on that superhighway at your right axillary lymph nodes," the surgeon explained. "Now it can travel all around your body. There are nodes in the clavicle, too, and in other clusters all over the body, but the axillary and clavicle are the most common places that breast cancer accesses the superhighway." He looked to me and then to Scott to see if we had any questions. We remained silent. "Chemotherapy will help stop any cancer cells that have jumped onto that superhighway before they can find a home in any other part of your body."

Understanding the function of the lymphatic system as a transportation network and breast cancer as a semi that can jump on at the hub of the axillary lymph nodes en route to other organs and body systems is frightening enough; understanding it in relation to the discovery of cancer cells within my own axillary lymph nodes made the day of this first meeting with the surgeon the single worst day among the collection of terrible days I had tallied up so far.

"What if it already has landed in another place in my body?" I asked. "What if it's too late to stop it before it jumps off somewhere else?"

"Answering that question is what comes next," he said.

CHAPTER EIGHT

Cancer staging is the process of determining how far a known cancer has spread inside a patient's body, though there is no guarantee of total accuracy. In situations of carcinoma-producing cancers, staging also aims to determine the size and quantity of the carcinomas the cancer has produced. There are four stages of cancer in total, and the final stage, stage 4, refers to cancer that has spread to other organs or body systems from the original location of the cancer; stage 4 is metastatic cancer.

Over the course of the month that followed the first appointment with my oncology surgeon, I underwent a series of diagnostic scans on the hunt for a landing place for any cancer cells that had originated in my breast and had grown into metastatic cancer of sufficient size that it could be detected elsewhere in my body.

The finding of cancer cells in my lymph nodes also offered up an additional mystery: where exactly did those nomadic cells originate? The cancer found in my initial biopsy was indisputably ductal carcinoma in situ—DCIS—which, by its definition and name, is stationary and cannot move to the nodes. As the surgeon had explained to Scott, we had backed into a discovery of invasive cancer. We knew the invasive cancer had to be somewhere in my breast since it had been found on the lymphatic superhighway in my axillary lymph nodes, but we had yet to diagnostically see an invasive breast cancer carcinoma in my breast tissue. Alongside a battery of diagnostic imaging that aimed to determine if the breast cancer had travelled farther than my lymph nodes, I also underwent imaging to find the invasive breast cancer carcinoma so that it could be measured and biopsied as well.

Throughout the month of June and into July, I didn't go a single week without returning to the Cancer Centre for a scan, blood work, or appointment of some kind. Neither my seven-year-old nor my four-year-old were oblivious to the number of appointments I suddenly had, so Scott and I decided to tell them a version of my diagnosis that they could digest at their young ages. They understood that I had an illness—cancer—and that I was going to meet with a lot of very skilled people to help me get rid of it. Giving them the word "cancer" as part of our explanation was an intentional choice made to reduce fear of an unknown and otherwise unnamed invader. As I began the process of cancer staging, this was as much as my kids knew regarding my diagnosis. Scott and I continued this approach for each step of my treatment path and had small conversations with them before big events, sharing the most important details with them and using all the proper terminology before encouraging them to ask any questions they had.

In mid-June, I had a standard MRI of my chest. This diagnostic test uses magnetic imaging to identify areas of dense tissue in the body as a potential space that cancer may be growing. In my case a dye, or contrast, was also administered to me via an IV, and two sets of images of my chest were taken. First, I lay face down on a small metal medical table that slid on rails to bring me underneath the portion of the machine that would take images of my chest. Next, the table slid back out from under the imaging portion of the machine so that a technologist could add dye into my veins via an

IV, then the table slid back under the machine for a second time. After the dye was introduced, my tissues and organs absorbed the new fluid now coursing through my bloodstream. When the pre- and post-injection images were compared, any changes in the literal brightness of the organs or tissues would indicate potential breast tumour sites. This standard MRI took around twenty minutes, during which the machine emitted a series of knocks and bangs varying in both volume and length as the spinning magnets captured images of my breast tissue. Despite remaining totally unmoving inside the MRI tunnel, the sounds of the machine gave me the overall feeling of being inside an industrial dryer.

Exactly one week later, in late June, I had a repeat MRI, this time with the addition of a biopsy. In a delightful and fortuitous turn of luck, the radiologist who was performing this second MRI and the additional biopsy was the same radiologist who had carried out my second ultrasound. The doctor who had insisted upon the immediate further investigation of my dense breast tissue with a mammogram was now the one who would be plumbing the depths of that same breast in order to deliver an exact diagnosis.

I was put into the MRI/dryer for images to be taken of my right breast, then removed for the contrast dye to be added to my bloodstream, then back into the dryer again for a second set of magnetically produced images. I remained on the table as still as possible as it slid in and out of the machine. My right breast was clamped in a vice-like device in order to reduce the possibility of movement as the radiologist reviewed the first and second sets of images captured during this MRI from the adjoining room.

"We have excellent imaging from both rounds, so I am going to start marking placement for the biopsy site," the radiologist spoke from somewhere behind and above me. Since I was pinned to the machine face down, I could not move to see her.

"How many spots lit up?" I asked.

"There are a few potential sites, and I've chosen the one that I feel is most likely to be a carcinoma based on the size and density shown by the scan," she replied to my back.

"Can you choose two? Double the likelihood of hitting the right area? This sucks and I don't want to go through this in vain," I reasoned. "I'm already here in this machine, so let's really go for it."

"Absolutely. I couldn't agree more," she said with confidence. "I will biopsy the two largest sites, one after the other. I like the idea of doubling the odds of success."

With this encouragement, the radiologist then sampled the two places within my breast that she had identified as potential harbours for the spectral invasive cancer within me. As the procedure was nearing completion, she told me that there would be a physical marker left behind at the biopsy sites in addition to the outwardly visible scars I would carry.

"There's a metal marker placed in the space of each biopsy site. They're used so that the exact origin of each sample can be identified in the pathology report and also in any future testing you have," she told me as she completed the second biopsy. "This way, the reports that come back will differentiate between the two samples and the location of both biopsy sites will be clearly identifiable on future imaging."

"So, there's a piece of metal in me now?" I asked. "Am I bionic?"

"That may be a stretch," she laughed. "It's an incredibly small marker! It can only be referenced when viewed on an x-ray and seen fully under a microscope."

"It will be identifiable after my breast is removed?" I asked, haltingly. "After my mastectomy?"

"Yes," she responded, "and we will know which tumour grew in which place, and exactly what type of cancer it was."

"All right," she said as the final biopsy was completed. She then bandaged up my second wound of the day and third to this breast within a month. "Let's get you out of this machine and back to your regular life."

As she helped me sit up, she turned to the nurse providing assistance throughout my procedure that day and asked him to go out to the waiting room down the hall and find Scott. When the nurse opened the door to the outer room, Scott was standing in the hallway immediately outside the door, a sentry waiting for me.

CHAPTER NINE

Over the course of four weeks, I'd had an MRI, an MRI-guided double biopsy, a bone scan, a fusion scan, and a CT scan. Each test was unique and awful in its own way. Some were quick, and some involved long periods of waiting; some necessitated IV injections before or during the test, and some required fasting. They all, however, involved me laying very still in a machine so that diagnostic images could be captured of my internal systems, organs, and bones while I thought about whether or not I was going to die. Then, I'd leave the machine and the hospital having no more answers than when I had left my oncology surgeon's office over a month prior. For four excruciating weeks I did not know if I was a terminal cancer patient growing carcinomas throughout my body or if I had pressed for more testing on my changing breasts within enough time to stop the cancer before it had a chance to metastasize.

This stretch of time was the lowest of the low for me. For four weeks in the summer of 2019, I was a ghost. Without exception, every time I had a conversation with someone over those four weeks I was simultaneously wondering where the results from my most recent test were. If I was talking with neighbours, I would wonder if there was an envelope with my name on it on my medical oncologist's desk. If I went to the library, I'd ask the librarian for books while also wondering if the tissue samples collected had finally found my elusive invasive cancer. I refused to make any plans that were not appointments directly related to my cancer staging and treatment, because if I was about to find out I was a terminal cancer patient I didn't want to have to cancel and explain why.

By the time I was entrenched in the process of staging my cancer, I had firmly transplanted myself from the position of Cancer Muggle with cancer to informed cancer patient. I now understood what each stage meant; where breast cancer was most likely to be found if it became metastatic, and thus what each individual diagnostic test was looking for; and that chemotherapy was unequivocally going to be both horrendous and something I was going to choose to do.

A few close friends knew I had experienced some changes in my body that needed investigating when I was sent for the ultrasound that successfully discovered my cancer. Within the whirlwind of time after meeting with my general practitioner in mid-May and learning that DCIS had been found, I had told more of my friends and family that I had been diagnosed with cancer and would likely be having surgery. The grapevine of family communication passed this news from one person to the next, eliminating the mental exhaustion I would have personally endured if I'd had to tell each person individually. Everybody was informed that this was a very early discovery necessitating minimal intervention. When it became clear to me that I was not going to get away from the cancer monster with such light sparring, I did not offer the updated news to anyone.

Close friends noticed that I suddenly had a lot of appointments at the Cancer Centre, but as Cancer Muggles themselves, no suspicions of a deeper issue seemed to have been planted and

I didn't tell a single person exactly what all these scans meant or what the outcome could be. It wasn't an intentional decision to keep my friends and family in the dark, it is just impossible to explain to a Cancer Muggle what all the terminology means to the depth that it could be understood sufficiently by someone not living it. The emotional toll it would take for me to explain repeatedly that I was facing either a very, very hard road or a potentially very short one was something I simply could not endure until I knew which road map I would be guided by.

Scott understood the crushing weight of this unknown, as he was there with me when I began to see the truest outlines of the beast I was battling. If he had not been at those early appointments I am not confident I would have been able to explain the weight of the cancer staging wait even to him. Cancer is a black hole that pulls every single aspect of life into it. It obliterated my ability to function in its presence and it systematically destroyed whatever came nearest to it in my life during the weeks I spent waiting to find out whether I was a terminal cancer patient. I am amazed that anyone wore clean clothing or ate food towards the end of this waiting period. Scott and I were both hollowed out with cracked shells by the time I finally, finally went in to meet with my oncology surgeon and receive the results of all those scans.

Over the course of less than two months, I'd endured:

Three ultrasounds
A mammogram
A mammogram biopsy
An MRI
An MRI-guided double biopsy
A bone scan
A fusion scan
A CT scan

"You've received the results of all the staging scans already, yes?" my oncology surgeon asked, almost off-hand as he walked into the examination room.

"What? No. I haven't heard anything," I replied, sliding from my sitting position on the exam table to stand on the floor in a hospital gown, my pants, and my socks. Suddenly I was without bones. I was somehow gelatin and frozen at once.

"Hang on, I'll get the pathology report," the surgeon said as he immediately turned around and disappeared back through the doorway.

Then he was gone and I knew that when he came back, I would know. Scott and I stared at each other, unable to speak. Listening to the clock tick, the office phone ring, people's footfalls as they walked the hallway outside the room where I was about to hear whether I was a terminal cancer patient.

When he came back in he had a shadow of a smile on his face and a folder of papers in his hand, but he didn't need to look at them to tell me the report results. Perhaps he had left to go get the detailed reports knowing I would want to read them line by line, but he must have known the staging results before he'd come into the exam room the first time.

"No cancer anywhere outside of your right breast and axillary lymph nodes," my stoic doctor calmly reported.

I was still stuck in front of the exam table, exactly where I landed when I'd slid off the table at his first question.

"FUCK YEAH!" I screamed. I screamed so loud that I am sure the medical staff and patients in other exam rooms heard me. Patients as far out as the waiting room are probably still telling their loved ones about the time someone in an inner examination room yelled "fuck" as loud as they could. This was a top-three moment for me on my list of cancer-patient highs, and I regret nothing.

I launched myself at my husband as he cried, and I cried.

My surgeon, ever the calm professional, merely said, "Yep, that's the appropriate response."

When I calmed down and stopped high-fiving the shit out of myself for waving at metastatic cancer but then walking away from it, we went over the imaging reports. One shadowy spot had been identified on my liver that necessitated investigating, but that was being undertaken out of an abundance of caution. I would undergo a liver ultrasound in mid-July that confirmed that there was nothing of concern.

On that day in the surgeon's examination room, I was classified as having stage 3, grade 3B breast cancer. The disease had jumped on the lymphatic superhighway but had not travelled anywhere else that could be found, and as long as nothing was discovered on my chest wall after my breasts were removed, I would remain stage 3 patient. There are four stages of cancer in total and the final stage, stage 4, refers to cancer that has spread to other organs or body systems from the original location of the cancer; stage 3 is not metastatic cancer.

PART TWO

chemotherapy

Life is a shipwreck but we must
not forget to sing in the lifeboats.

– VOLTAIRE

CHAPTER TEN

Exactly one week after meeting with the surgeon and yelling "Fuck yeah!" to everyone within earshot, I had my first meeting with my medical oncologist. The medical oncologist is the doctor who plans the medical treatments a cancer patient receives and is often the doctor who refers a patient to an oncology surgeon and a radiation oncologist whenever the timing is appropriate based upon the cancer involved. The specific treatments a medical oncologist could consider for a patient include chemotherapy, daily prescriptions, and long-term medications. The medical oncologist is also often the doctor who co-ordinates the regular screening of areas that a patient has already had cancer in, as well as diagnostic testing if any concerning symptoms arise elsewhere in a person's body.

The meeting with my medical oncologist was the first time anyone really laid it on the line for me as far as chemotherapy went. I had the bullet points from the discussion with my oncology surgeon during which I'd discovered that I would have to consider chemotherapy, but this was the first time I'd met with the oncologist who would be prescribing the cocktail of medications in my particular regime. Yes, I would lose all my hair. Yes, I would be unwell, though in what specific ways no one could say for certain. Yes, I would be severely immunocompromised for a period of time during each round of chemo. But, yes, I could do this.

After I was called into the examination room, I changed into the thin hospital gown and sat on the freshly unrolled paper spread across the examination table. My medical oncologist came in minutes later and introduced herself. She confirmed that I had already received the news of my stage 3 status and we then immediately discussed the additional information that had been provided by the most recent biopsy I underwent, the one guided by an MRI.

"I understand that the discovery of cancer in my lymph nodes means that I need to do chemotherapy. The surgeon described it as 'finding the footprints of invasive cancer before the discovery of the tumour,'" I said as I slipped off my boots and curled my legs under me on the narrow table. "What was the purpose of the MRI biopsy if we already knew there was more than just DCIS in my breast? Why go through that?"

"That's a valid question. It would seem like an unnecessary test if invasive cancer was already evident," she admitted. "The more important reason for requesting the additional biopsy was so that your breast cancer could be typed. Knowing the exact type of cancer that you have is crucial in determining the chemotherapy medications that will best target your cancer," she explained.

"I assumed breast cancer was breast cancer. There are different types?" Scott asked.

"For a long time that was presumed to be the case, but as understanding of cancer advances, we now know that that is not true. The wide variety of breast cancer types is why two people that have cancer in the same location can approach that diagnosis with wildly differing treatment paths," said the oncologist. "Two patients could have breast cancer by general diagnosis; however, if the type and stage of cancer they have is not identical, it might look like two different diseases to someone comparing only their treatment plans. Also, age can play a role in determining which medications are administered, even if the type and stage of the cancer are the same. There are many factors to consider."

"Did the MRI finally find an invasive tumour? Or maybe I should refer to it as the evasive tumour," I asked. "The radiologist biopsied two places to increase the likelihood of finding it."

"The biopsy was successful in sampling an invasive carcinoma," the doctor replied. "The type found is estrogen and progesterone positive, HER2-negative cancer. This means that your invasive carcinomas thrive in the presence of the hormones estrogen and progesterone."

"Carcinomas?" I repeated, unsure if my ringing ears had heard her intricate descriptors correctly or if cancer trauma was obscuring my memory in real time. "There was cancer found in both places during the biopsy?" I asked.

How much cancer can one breast hold?

"That's correct. Both MRI biopsy sites found cancer, but the number of tumours doesn't have a significant correlation with severity when they are in the same organ and are of the same type of cancer, which both of these are," she replied.

I audibly exhaled at the news that having more than one carcinoma did not correlate with a certain death sentence.

"Some breast cancers are estrogen positive but progesterone negative; a very small number of breast cancers are estrogen negative but progesterone positive; and still others are negative for both," she continued. "Knowing how your specific cancer reacts in the presence of hormones is a vital piece of information that those biopsies successfully provided. This knowledge dictates the types of chemotherapy that will be included in your treatment regime, it suggests additional surgeries that you will have to consider, and it also dictates the types of ongoing medications I will prescribe during the years after you finish active treatment," she concluded.

"Hitting the mark during that MRI biopsy was more important than I understood at the time," I reflected, doubly grateful in retrospect that I had pushed for two biopsy sites.

"I can't overstate how important this piece of diagnostics is," my medical oncologist reiterated.

Later, when I'm back at home, I read much deeper into those library books I'd neglected in previous weeks, and I learned much more about hormones, and how they can affect breast cancer. The driving force behind the human reproductive system is hormones and the presence of estrogen is vital for people that have a uterus and ovaries if they wish to release an egg that can then be fertilized. Since my carcinoma thrived in an estrogen-rich environment, it now made sense that the density in my breast would become more pronounced right before and during ovulation. While my body was creating an environment conducive to life by increasing estrogen production before I ovulated, it was simultaneously creating an environment conducive to my own death by feeding my carcinoma with the hormone that put its cellular dividing and conquering skills on overdrive.

"What about that other part? Something was negative as well?" I asked the oncologist.

"Yes. The final piece of cancer typing information that the biopsy provided was to determine your HER2 status. HER2 refers to the human epidermal growth factor receptor 2 gene, which can contribute to the growth and development of some breast cancers," explained the doctor. "In the case of a HER2-positive breast cancer, the HER2 gene essentially becomes a photocopier with the copy button stuck down. The HER2 gene makes more and more copies of a HER2 protein, in essence copying its own abnormality, and this copying repeats over and over again until the cells are growing in an uncontrolled way."

"Ashleigh doesn't have this broken gene though, right? If her cancer tested negative for it, then the HER gene isn't contributing to cancer growth?" Scott wondered aloud.

"Right," she replied, "HER2 is not a factor in this case."

"Is that better? To be negative for HER2? Or estrogen positive? Is there any preferred combination of all of these factors?" I asked, desperate for some sliver of silver lining in this thunderstorm.

"Each combination has its unique benefits and unique difficulties," she admitted. "HER2-positive breast cancer tends to be aggressive and spread quickly; however, it also tends to respond quickly and favourably to chemotherapy medications that target the HER2 protein and stop it from multiplying all over the breast. In a similar way, hormone-positive cancers have specific treatments that can be effective at reducing growth." She paused here to let this contrasting example sink in. "Hormones can be slowed, and they can be eliminated," she finished.

"So, each type sucks in its own special way," Scott offered.

"In short, yes," she confirmed with a smile.

"So, I have stage 3, estrogen-positive, HER2-negative breast cancer," I summarized.

"Your full diagnosis at this point is stage 3, grade 3B, estrogen and progesterone-positive, HER2-negative multifocal invasive mammary carcinoma," she corrected. "Try to say that three times fast."

Scott and I smirked at the impossibility of saying—let alone truly emotionally absorbing—the type of cancer I have.

After all the explanations of positives and negatives, we moved on to discuss the specific chemotherapy medications I would be receiving. The exact regime of chemotherapy medications that I would receive was called TAC, which stands for Taxotere®/ Adriamycin®/cyclophosphamide. The plan for me was to do six rounds of the same chemo cocktail consisting of one dose of each medication administered every three weeks. My medical oncologist was upfront from the very beginning that it would not be easy on me. The TAC chemotherapy mix was generally repeated six times only for young and otherwise healthy patients because of how severely it could devastate all non-cancerous body systems and organs.

Now I had a treatment plan laid out by my medical oncologist that was informed by the pathology of my carcinomas. Over the course of the next three hours, each individual chemotherapy medication I would receive was explained to me along with the exact steps I would have to take in preparation for treatment to begin. Chemotherapy would start right away and I was told to expect a call within a few days with an appointment for my first infusion. Once again, that speed amplification factor was highlighting exactly how important it was to stop the cancer progression immediately.

CHAPTER ELEVEN

During my marathon appointment with the medical oncologist I learned that Taxotere—the T of my TAC chemotherapy regimen—is the primary culprit of hair loss, and it also has a tendency to make the scalp hypersensitive. My oncologist shared with me that over her years in practice, she'd had patients who waited for their hair to begin falling out before shaving their heads and then they reported having a more discomforting experience because the pulling and pressure from clippers aggravated their hypersensitive scalps. I wasn't interested in going anywhere farther than my own bathroom to lose my hair, and I also preferred choosing the exact moment that I would be bald as opposed to examining the shower drain every day waiting for evidence of a follicle attack. I wanted to be bald on my own terms, even if the change was ultimately unavoidable; therefore, a few days before my first chemotherapy treatment, Scott shaved my head.

I sat on a chair in our bathroom while he gathered up my hair in his hand and cut it close to my scalp with scissors while I practiced steadily breathing in and out. Ava shaved the first section of my hair down to about two centimetres with clippers while I cried. Right up until that very moment, I had expected that losing my hair would be a relatively insignificant event. In the scheme of what I had to face it was minor; however, in that moment I was near inconsolable. Until the point of shaving my head, I moved about in life as a person with cancer, but it was not visible. Those who were in the know regarding my deadly illness were there because I had chosen to disclose my diagnosis to them. In addition to my immediate family, a handful of my closest friends were the only people to know how the lymphatic superhighway had altered my staging. Fundamentally, I largely had control over who would and would not know that I was dealing with a life-threatening illness because all the evidence of that illness was on the inside of me. There are many reasons why a mid-thirties female-presenting adult could have a buzz cut besides cancer, but cancer is certainly one of the first reasons that comes to people's minds and I was not thrilled about being a cancer patient who looked like a cancer patient.

After Scott and our kids had shorn my hair down close to my head and I looked at my new reflection for the first time, it finally, finally felt very real that I was a cancer patient at the utter beginning of a largely unknown road into hell. I was not a Cancer Muggle any longer. I was certainly no oncologist, but I had a deeper and wider knowledge of breast cancer treatments than most average people at this point. What I did not yet have within me was the visceral, physical knowledge of what it is like to receive chemotherapy and what would happen to my own body and mind before, during, and after accepting those medications. That would come very soon, but the day Scott shaved my head in our bathroom was the apex of the most educated I was and the most personally inexperienced I would ever be regarding cancer treatment. At this point, only two months after first hearing the word "cancer," I was strangely looking forward to beginning the most significant step in vanquishing the disease in my body.

CHAPTER TWELVE

"Are you ready?" Scott asked me as we walked once again from the parking lot towards the Cancer Centre. It was late July of 2019 and the day that I would officially become an "active" cancer patient. It was the day of my first administration of chemotherapy.

"Physically? Yes," I replied. "I took the third dose of steroids this morning, so I guess I am as prepared as I can make myself to avoid rejecting the meds."

"The steroids are those small white pills you took yesterday, too?"

"Yeah, that's them. Dexa . . . something," I replied. "They reduce the possibility of chemo rejection, but they also eliminate the possibility of sleep. My heart was racing and my eyes stayed wide open all night," I complained. "I mean, the fact that I am here today to receive an IV smoothie of cytotoxic drugs didn't exactly rock me into a gentle slumber last night, either, I guess."

"I don't think I slept either," Scott lamented as we neared the front lobby of the Cancer Centre. "Do you take them again tonight?"

"Yeah, tonight and then again tomorrow, too."

We entered the now familiar Cancer Centre waiting room and

I was quickly registered for my appointment. We made our way downstairs and to a section of the medical facility that we had not yet visited—the waiting room for patients receiving chemotherapy.

My name was called mid-morning, and Scott and I passed through the two swinging doors labelled "Chemotherapy and Medical Day Care" and into the chemotherapy unit for the first time. The largest section of the room was wide open with hospital beds and reclining chairs facing each other across a rectangle of floor space, anchored at the corner by the nurses' station. Each chair and bed had tracking secured to the ceiling above so that a curtain could be drawn around a patient in the event privacy was needed. There was also a large collection of regular chairs positioned all around the room, many occupied by a person sitting beside someone in a bed. Around the bend at the nurses' station, the smaller section of the L-shaped chemotherapy unit housed two washrooms labelled as being "Exclusively for Chemotherapy Patient Usage," as well as several beds that had three walls around them and a curtain at the foot. I followed the nurse who had called my name to a hospital bed in the corner of the room closest to the nurses' station and sat on the bed with nervous anticipation.

Before I'd had time to properly exhale, I recognized my mismatch with the demographic of the patients receiving treatment in the room. I was thirty-five and the majority of people attached to IV trees appeared to be in their sixties. Some were clearly much older, but not one patient appeared to be even in their forties, much less as young as thirty-five. Walking into the chemotherapy unit felt as though someone pushed me unwillingly onto a stage and directly into the spotlight. Almost as soon as I sat down on the bed, the patient next to me leaned over Scott and told me that I was far too young to be there.

"I agree," I said with a smile.

"Is this really happening?" I asked Scott, turning to face him.

He looked like a deer caught in the headlights of the gaze of everyone around us, just like me.

"Unbelievable as it is, yes," he replied.

I reached up and removed the scarf I had wrapped around my shorn scalp.

"I suppose if I am ever going to rock a bald head, this is the best place to do it," I assessed. "Maybe it will actually help me blend in better here, since I appear to be the youngest patient by at least two decades."

"You were a magnetic pull for all the eyes when we came in. I could see people looking at you as if you were a child entering the room," he told me quietly, as to not be overheard in the open unit.

"I suppose I represent to these fellow cancer patients what a bald child in a hospital room would represent to us," I replied, equally as quiet, as I looked around the room and took in all the other patients sitting on their own beds or in reclining chairs. "I am a cellular tragedy."

"Ashleigh?" asked a nurse as she approached my bed.

"That's me," I confirmed.

"I'm your nurse today. Since it's your first chemotherapy treatment, we prefer to put you in a bed in case you have a reaction to any of the meds you'll receive. Do you have your port yet?" she asked while pulling a blood pressure machine towards me and pointing at my mouth with the end of a thermometer, indicating I should open up. These statements, questions, and instructions poured from her in the steady stream of a nurse working on muscle memory.

I shook my head to say no as Scott answered for me. I was unable to speak with the thermometer under my tongue.

"No, that's in a few weeks," he told her. I was scheduled to have a port-a-cath surgically inserted in my chest in mid-August, two weeks away. Once the port was implanted, medications could be delivered directly into an artery above my heart, bypassing my veins. For the first round of chemo, it would be administered through the IV at my hand. The nurse inserted a cannula into the back of my right hand as she began walking me through the medications I would receive and what their purposes were.

"Did you take every dose of dexamethasone you were prescribed?" she asked as she hooked a bag of clear fluid on the IV tree behind me. "That's the steroid you need to take before chemotherapy."

"Yes," I confirmed. "Third dose this morning, and I have three more waiting at home."

"Excellent," she replied. "I'm going to start you on the first medication now as we wait for the chemotherapy drugs to be dispensed from Central Pharmacy," she finished hooking lines up to the cannula in my hand as she said this.

"This isn't chemotherapy?" I pointed to the bag on the IV tree as I asked.

"The first two medications administered are antiemetics—or antinausea medications—which will help make you feel less nauseous," she explained.

"Just less nauseous?" I asked. "Not eliminate the nausea, just reduce it?"

"Exactly," she replied. She either did not pick up on my sarcasm or was foreshadowing the nausea experience I was in for in the coming days, and I didn't wish to press her to determine which scenario was correct.

The nurse continued, "Each chemotherapy medication carries with it some side effects that are more likely to occur and others that are less likely, though there are no guarantees for any of them. We try to get ahead of the nausea that all of the medications that you will receive today cause by giving you two different kinds of antiemetics even before the chemotherapy begins." She had finished connecting the IV line in my hand with the one snaking down from the loops above the IV pump and then turned away from me to activate the pump. The liquid began to drip, drip, drip into the lines, and I watched as the fluid slowly and steadily moved downward through the silicone tube towards the needle in my hand. Within seconds it reached the loops taped to my skin and entered my vein.

The nurse had administered this medication countless times to countless patients and she carried on with her explanation as I assumed she had many times before while I remained frozen in that moment, witnessing my own body receive cancer-fighting medications for the first time.

It took well over an hour to drain the liquid from each of the first two bags and I was also given saline between each medication to flush out the lines of my IV. Early in the afternoon, the same nurse returned holding a new bag filled with liquid—my first dose of chemotherapy.

"Chemotherapy medications work by attacking rapidly dividing cells in the body; however, cancer cells are not the only cells that our bodies contain that divide rapidly," she explained. "Hair follicles are collections of rapidly dividing cells, and nail beds are as well," she carried on. "Have you discussed cold therapy with your oncologist?"

"No," I admit.

"We can talk about the possibility of adding that to your day now," she reassured me. "Because chemotherapy is delivered by the blood to all parts of the body, if a body part is made cold while chemo is being administered, it will receive less blood flow and, hopefully, that body part will be exposed to a less intense concentration of the medication."

"So, I should just be freezing while getting chemotherapy?" I asked.

"If your whole body is freezing, how do you know the chemo is getting to the places where the cancer is?" Scott queried, looking at me but directing the question to the nurse.

"We need to be strategic about the cold therapy," the nurse answered us both. "For your regime, the Taxotere is particularly harsh on hair follicles and nail beds."

"My oncologist told me that the T is going to cause my hair to fall out."

"They will probably all contribute, but it's inescapable with Taxotere. Losing your fingernails and toenails is also possible," she informed us.

"Fuck right off," I replied.

"Yep. In addition to being uncomfortable, a missing nail is a significant infection risk for a person already immunocompromised, so we'd really like to prevent that from happening," she further explained. "I'm going to bring some pans filled with ice after I begin the first chemotherapy drug, and I want you to put one hand in each pan far enough to submerge all your fingertips in the ice."

"So hopefully the chemotherapy will not make it all the way to the end of my fingers and I will keep my fingernails?" I predicted.

"Bingo," she responded.

"Do I only need to do that for one medication?" I asked.

"Just the Taxotere," she confirmed.

These kind and patient explanations from my chemotherapy nurse are why I sat with my hands in ice cold water for an hour while receiving the Taxotere. The hope of preventing the drug from causing my fingernails to fall off was at the top of my mind; however, it was about as comfortable as one would imagine it is to sit in a hospital bed with all ten fingers submerged in two kidney-shaped bowls filled with ice. The ice melted multiple times, and Scott had to drain out the water as it accumulated and refill the ice more than once before the IV bag was emptied. I would take my fingers out and warm them every few minutes because it was just so damned cold.

By the time I was nearing the end of the bag of Taxotere, I had been in the chemotherapy department for nearly five hours and I'd received three medications via IV. The discomfort of receiving the medications through a cannula in my hand was wearing on me, and I knew I still had two more medications to get through, plus the saline flushing that followed every medication. The IV tree that held the bags of liquid medication was stationed behind me and in the mid-afternoon it began beeping to alert the nursing staff that I had just polished off the final drips of Taxotere. I removed my frigid fingertips from the pans of ice, dried them on a towel, and sat waiting for the second medication of my TAC regime to be hooked up.

The nurse came to my bedside, and this time, instead of holding a translucent bag visibly filled with liquid, she was holding a small opaque bag made of brown plastic. I did not track this difference immediately though because the nurse herself was also approaching the delivery of this medication in a substantially different manner. If you look up any iteration of "what is the harshest chemotherapy" it will assuredly list Adriamycin at or near the top. The effectiveness of the A medication in my TAC chemo cocktail is largely due to its potency as a literal poison to all living cells, and it is because of its malevolent nature that receiving Adriamycin is a unique experience within the overall shit show of chemotherapy. The nurse was wearing gloves, a paper scrub set including booties covering her regular shoes, and a surgical mask.

"This is . . . intense," I commented.

"Intense and also necessary to protect my body in the event that the medication leaks out of the syringe," she explained.

"Syringe? It doesn't drip in the IV like the others?" I asked, fully confused.

The nurse sat beside me on the bed and pulled her mask down from her mouth so she could better communicate with Scott and me. She pulled the perforated tab on the brown bag that contained my second chemotherapy medication, reached inside, and pulled out what can only be described as a comically giant syringe filled with bright red liquid.

"This is Adriamycin, also called doxorubicin, but to those that administer or receive it, it is often just 'The Red Devil,'" she shared, smiling. "If this medication leaks from the bag and lands on my body, it would burn my skin. That's why I wear extra layers of protective clothing when I am administering it into your IV. Even the bag is specialized—it's made of a UV-blocking material since Adriamycin is photosensitive, meaning light can break it down."

"So, it would burn skin but you are going to inject it into my hand? Sounds like a plan!" I quipped, a sure sign of my own acquiescence to the insanity and absurdity of life as a cancer patient. "Why isn't it going to be attached to that?" I asked, pointing to the IV tree behind me with the hand attached to the line snaking down the pole.

"Because The Red Devil is so caustic, it cannot safely be administered via a standard plastic bag on an IV tree. The administration must be monitored constantly for the entire time that it is being given, and to do that I am going to administer it by hand from the syringe directly into your IV line," she explained. "That way I can watch as it is going into the lines attached to your body and ensure that not a drop spreads out under your skin or lands on you. It also means I can control the rate of delivery and ensure that it does not get introduced to your system too quickly."

I was at an absolute loss for words. This nurse was on the precipice of pressing the plunger on this Acme-style syringe filled with poison fruit punch while sitting beside me and alternating between staring at the place where the evil entered the line I was attached to and the place where the line deposited the evil into my body, all while dressed in a chemotherapy-unit spacesuit. The only thing I could do was laugh at the absurdity of the situation, at the fact that this chaos was about to be swirling around inside my body.

"Why is it bright red?" Scott asked her.

"A dye is added to make it easier for the person administering it to be absolutely certain where the liquid is at all times," she replied.

"Smart. I guess," he conceded.

"It's a fairly quick process for this one, not the hour-long drip of the first medication," she further explained. "I'll get it started now and with a steady pressure on the syringe it will likely be empty in twenty minutes or so," she concluded. "Should we get started?"

"Let's rock" I said. "Well, actually, first can you unplug my IV from the wall? I need to go pee . . . again," I said.

Hours earlier in the day, I'd discovered why those two bathrooms were labelled as exclusively for patients receiving chemotherapy. Not only is it because everything that came out of us was toxic and it's wise to keep that output contained to a few designated bathrooms, but also because the cancer patients around the room formed a caravan heading to the bathrooms all day long. Every one of us was hooked up to our own IV pump dispensing medications to battle our own type of cancer, and those medications were all liquid. Litres and litres of liquid medications along with at least one litre of saline were entering the bloodstream of each patient and it all had to come back out. Every time a patient in the chemotherapy unit needed to dispose of some of that residual liquid, we'd get our IV tree unplugged from the wall and pull it along with us for a visit to the bathroom. While unplugged, the IV pump would constantly beep to indicate that it was running on battery power and to encourage the user to plug it back in. Before my first dance with The Red Devil, I hoisted myself up from the bed, rolled my slender beeping companion into the too-small bathroom, and relieved myself. When I returned, Scott aided me in getting disentangled from my IV lines and then plugged my IV pump back in as I settled onto the bed.

Adriamycin in, another saline flush, on to the next medication.

Following the hand-delivery of The Red Devil, the final chemotherapy medication seemed almost normal. The "C" in my chemotherapy alphabet of awful stood for cyclophosphamide, and luckily this medication did not require any modifications while being administered. I got to sit on my hospital bed and contemplate the series of events that had led me so swiftly to be receiving chemotherapy while the bag of medication dripped into my veins without any distraction provided by icy fingers or nurses in medical spacesuits.

More than seven hours after it had begun, my IV pump beeped down its timer for the last time and I was unhooked from the lines and free to go home. Scott and I left the chemotherapy unit as fast as humanly possible, and the smell of the fresh air and the feeling of a light breeze on my face after a day on the road into the unknown consequences of chemotherapy was the sweetest sensory experience of my life.

"I've never been so delighted to see a parking lot," Scott said as we crossed to our vehicle in the dusky summer evening.

"I couldn't agree more," I whispered.

"How are you?" Scott asked. I knew he was not simply asking about how my body felt at that moment, though he was asking that, but also how my mind was coping with the events of the runaway train that had been the previous two months.

"Two months ago I didn't even know I had cancer," I quietly replied, my body swimming in toxicity.

"You still had it then, you just didn't know it," he countered.

"My hand is sore," I reported, rubbing my wrist, "I guess from being held in one position by the IV for so long. It's also itchy from the medical tape." I looked at my hand, red and bumpy, and then over at Scott's face filled with equal portions of love and worry and pride.

How do *I feel?*

"I feel all right. I feel more emotionally wrung out than physically, though maybe I'll regret saying that tomorrow. I'm doing all right at this moment," I concluded as he took my backpack off my shoulder and put it across his own. I slipped my arm into his and we walked in a comfortable quiet back to our car.

That night, I took my plethora of medications prescribed for the day of chemotherapy, and on that night not even the dose of steroids could keep my eyelids open.

At the end of my first day as an active cancer patient, all four of us—Scott, our two kids and myself—went to sleep together in our big family bed.

CHAPTER THIRTEEN

The day after my first chemotherapy treatment was a Wednesday. As I was dressing that morning, I performed the breast exam that I had carried out so many times since my initial finding of a mass, and that day, for the first time, there was a dramatic change: the mass was softer.

"Scott!" I yelped, still standing half-dressed in our ensuite bathroom. I heard the clatter of whatever he was holding being dropped in the main bathroom across the hallway followed by urgent footsteps echoing as he raced into the bedroom towards the ensuite.

"Are you okay?" he gasped.

"I . . . feel," I said.

Scott placed a flat palm on top of the densest segment of my breast. His hand barely grazed the top of the portion where the carcinoma was located when his eyes widened with glee.

"Holy shit," he choked out, stunned.

"This isn't possible."

"It's different!" he exclaimed, not an iota of doubt in his voice or his eyes. "It changed. I can feel it. Fuck, I can practically see the change!" He took a step backwards to assess the mass, further emphasizing the magnitude of change evident.

"We're desperately wishing to see a difference. We're looking for a sign," I countered.

"Just because you look for one and find one, it doesn't mean it's not true."

Damn, he's wise.

In one night—less than twenty-four hours—the carcinoma in my right breast had undergone a noticeable change. This change would repeat itself again the next morning and the morning after that as the density of my right breast lessened and lessened. By the fourth day after the first chemotherapy treatment, the mass had softened enough that, for the first time in months, there was a definite area of soft tissue at the top of my breast. Up until I had started chemotherapy, it had felt as though the carcinoma had been taking up all the space in my breast right up to the skin. Now, the trespasser was being diminished so that the softer, average breast tissue filled up the space that the cancer was vacating. It could not be denied—this seemed like evidence that the chemotherapy was rolling through the cells in my body and already evicting the cancerous interlopers.

Back on that first day after chemotherapy, once Scott left for work, my kids and I carried on with our plan for an easy day at home. Prior to starting the chemotherapy regime, Scott and I had filled Ava and Bean in on the very basics of what would be happening—I was going to receive medication at the hospital that would hopefully make the cancer go away, but that might also make me feel really tired and maybe sick too—with the goal of letting them know that all plans in the coming months would bend, change, and break in any way chemotherapy demanded. It was the first day after the first treatment, but my kids already understood that chemotherapy had become the fifth member of our family. I remained hypervigilant for any signs of nausea over the course of the day, and I took my prescribed antinausea medications every four or six hours as instructed by their labels.

Once chemotherapy had begun, my oncologists wanted to keep to the timeline of administering a dose every three weeks. I could not receive chemotherapy treatments if I was devastatingly immunocompromised, so I'd have to have blood work to measure my red and white blood cell counts as well as my platelet levels several days prior to each infusion. To help prevent missing a dose of chemotherapy due to low white blood cell levels, at two days post-chemo, I gave myself an injection in the fatty tissue around my belly button. The medication would help boost my white blood cell count by forcing my bones to speed up the process of producing the cells and releasing them into my blood.

The injection itself was relatively painless and I was outfitted with everything I needed to be able to administer it at home in the days after chemotherapy. The effect, however, was pain in my leg and hip bones so intense and deep that I was unable to walk down the hallway of my home the day after the injection. If you have never experienced bone pain, it's as if the insides of your bones are trying to escape from your body but the outsides of your bones won't allow it. All parts of the large bones in the body are fighting on a side of this escape and the constant clenching caused by these opposing forces makes the muscles around those bones fatigued and crampy within hours of the bone pain starting. As the pain continued on for days, I couldn't help but clench my jaw and hike my shoulders, causing muscle aches in other parts of my body as well. It was swell.

As if the physical pain wasn't enough, the injection also isn't covered by Newfoundland's Medical Care Plan. Each single injection cost $1,978.28 at the time I was receiving it, and it has probably gone up in cost since writing this sentence. Miraculously, our private medical plan covered eighty per cent of the cost of this medication; however, I would be receiving the injection six times in five months and the financial burden remaining for my family was significant. I am extremely fortunate that I was able to access a compassionate cost offset program through the Cancer Centre that some drug manufacturers participate in; however, the astronomically high price tag of some medications is prohibitive for many, many cancer patients.

In the days surrounding the beginning of the most rigorous medical intervention of my life, the last thing I should have had to worry about was securing the financial means to pay for the medications that would contribute to my ability to follow the chemotherapy regime set out before me, yet because we do not have universal pharmacare in Canada, that's exactly what I was doing.

Four days after administering the injection, the bone pain finally began to lessen, though I knew it was temporary relief, as I would be administering another one in just a few weeks. One week out from my first dance with chemotherapy, I felt normal. The worst of my symptoms could best be described as the feeling you have when you've had the flu but you can sense that you're recovering. My bounce back was propelled by the mounting evidence of an effective chemotherapy response I experienced in the diminishing denseness in my breast.

If this is what chemo will do, I can handle it for the next five months.

CHAPTER FOURTEEN

At ten days post-chemo, I felt sufficiently recovered to attend a weekly get-together with several other families that also homeschool their kids. Our homeschool co-op is a staple in the lives of my family, and I consider the group of kids and parents in the three other families that make up our homeschool co-op to be among my family's closest friends. Once chemotherapy became foundational on my road away from cancer, I knew that regular attendance with our co-op would be impossible, so I was happy to be able to attend a gathering just over a week after my first cycle.

It was a beautiful day in early August when we moved from the backyard of our host family to a green space behind their home, and it was while sitting on the grass watching my kids run around with their friends on that warm morning that I realized my hair was falling out. After my buzz cut, I was not comfortable being out in public with a bare head, so I began experimenting with wrapping my head in scarves any time I left the house. I reached up to the divot above my ear to adjust my head wrap, thinking the tag on the scarf I was wearing that day was making my temple itch. When I brought my hand back down, it was covered in short hairs that had fallen out of my scalp at the slightest touch of my fingertips. I reached up to my scalp again, found a larger pinch of hair at the back of my neck and tugged it. I felt nothing but was rewarded with a handful of hair. It was all falling out. I knew that the short hair remaining after my family had cut off the length was all but guaranteed to fall out, yet this was still an especially painful gut punch, and I calmly but swiftly gathered my kids to leave. Once we were buckled into the car, I explained to them why I needed to go home and showed them how I could remove handfuls of my hair with ease. I sobbed all the way home as I drove.

That evening, I stood on the back deck of my home and brushed my hands across my scalp over and over as a torrent of small hairs fell to the ground. The physical act of losing my hair felt like absolutely nothing. If I had not seen the hairs on my own hands, if I had not had the ability to look at my reflection in the mirror that night before bed and see that I was now totally bald, I would not have believed that my hair was gone. Shortly after the hair on my head fell out, the hair on my arms and legs began disappearing as well.

As if I hadn't experienced enough body dysmorphia already, eleven days after my body hair began its exodus, I had a port-a-cath implanted in my chest. A port-a-cath, or port for short, is a purple triangle made of silicone about the diameter of a toonie but three centimetres thick that sits completely under the skin around the collarbone. The part that faces outward from the body has a slit in the silicone that can be accessed by a needle to draw blood or to administer medication to the body. Underneath my skin, the access port was attached to a silicone line that circled up alongside my neck and then back down into a vein leading directly into my heart. The port placement procedure is routine, but for me it was another significant leap into the identity of a cancer patient. I was awake the whole time and it took less than an hour from the time I arrived at the hospital until the device was implanted and I was heading home.

I'd never had anything implanted in my body before and the feeling of pressure immediately after the implant surgery was unnerving. Having a mole removed or a tooth extracted were experiences I'd had, but the absence of something that used to be there is a very different bodily sensation compared to the addition of something that was not previously there. The information packet that I was given after the procedure contained a serial number for my specific device as well as a card to put in my wallet in case of an emergency so that medical professionals would know exactly what implanted device I had, where it was, and how long it had been there. I left the hospital with two small incisions and a huge purple triangle under my skin, and I went home to prepare for cycle number two of chemotherapy, which would be happening the very next day.

The nearly $2,000 injection and bevy of anti-nausea medications and steroids waiting in my cupboard were the same this time as the last; differentiating this cycle was the person accompanying me for the day. I had tolerated the first administration of chemotherapy well and I felt I knew what to expect, so for the second cycle, Scott went to work and one of my closest friends, Becca, would be there with me all day. Becca's presence was the singular reason Scott felt comfortable not accompanying me, and yet even given this plan he second-guessed himself multiple times prior to the appointment.

I met Becca at fourteen years old when her parents and siblings moved back to Newfoundland after spending a few years in Indonesia. Becca was the maid of honour at my wedding, and she was the first person Scott and I called when we found out we were going to be parents, both times. Becca, her husband, and their two kids now lived in a different province than my family; however, once the writing was on the wall regarding my treatment plan, she insisted that she would be there with me in person for a cycle of chemotherapy to support me in any way that she could. Becca and her kids arrived to stay for a week and a half at her parents' home just prior to the start of my second chemotherapy cycle. She travelled over 3,000 kilometres just so she could sit beside me in a plastic hospital chair for seven hours and watch me try to poison just enough of my cells to live. Becca drained and refilled my ice pans, untangled my IV lines every time I had to pee, and laughed in horror along with me when the nurse in a spacesuit came to inject The Red Devil into my chest.

"How are you managing?" Becca asked me towards the midpoint of the day of chemotherapy.

"I'm tired," I replied. "More tired than last time."

"It's oddly exhausting to sit and do so little," she commiserated.

"Isn't it!" I laughed. "Actually, I just realized that I feel a lot like I did on the day after chemo last time. Sort of like I was coming down with something."

"There's a lot going on inside you right now. And around you," Becca reminded me.

"Yeah. I viscerally recall this combination of anxiety, fatigue, and also restlessness from last time," I said. "But it was the next day. This is much quicker."

"You're allowed to rest and not overanalyze," Becca counselled me as she held my hand.

"I love you, dear friend," I replied, as I took her advice immediately and fell asleep, waking only sporadically throughout the remainder of the afternoon.

I was experiencing the compacting effect of chemotherapy. I felt okay after the first treatment because I was healthy, aside from having all that cancer. The second time that I accepted chemotherapy, I had a little less cancer but I was also a little less healthy.

The nature of riding the chemotherapy roller coaster is that you never climb quite as far back up after each plummet downwards, and eventually you just bottom-out and stay down. The second cycle of chemo hit me harder and sooner, and this pattern would repeat with every cycle afterwards.

I wasn't able to drive after the chemo cycle was completed, so Becca drove me and my car home. Despite a hundred texts exchanged with me, and then later additional updates exchanged with Becca, I could sense that Scott was anxious to be home and with me as soon as possible. I went to bed almost as soon as I got in the door after cycle number two, and as our kids ate he came to the bedside to debrief on the day.

"I hated not being there," he began. "I could hardly concentrate all day, even with all the texts. Once Becca started texting me to say you were asleep, I knew I'd made the wrong choice."

"You know she took excellent care of me. She's the only other person I would have wanted there," I assured him, sleep descending over my body and voice.

"I know she did. I don't question that at all," he reported. "I wanted to be there for me, not because I was afraid you were lacking in care. I'd bet Becca knows where the blanket warmer is and how to go get more ice for the pans just as confidently as I do now."

"I confirm she does know just the right moment to empty and refill the ice pans," I told him quietly with a smile. The comedic uniqueness of these moments was not lost on me, even as the burden of all the medications fighting for dominance within my body began to accumulate to the point of total exhaustion.

"She's also going home in a week," I reminded Scott.

"That's why I already booked off all of the remaining chemo days," he informed me.

"That was the right choice," I replied as I turned to my side and closed my eyes. I felt him take my glasses and lay them at the bedside before he left the room.

Recovery after round two was markedly different than after round one. I spent the entirety of the day afterwards near my bed and, while I did not actually vomit, I counted down the half hours all day long so I could take my next dose of my antinausea medications right on time. Becca came back every day that week and took my kids to the playground, played with them around the house, and probably did our laundry while she was there. On day two, I once again administered the harbinger of bone pain into my middle and doubled down on my daily dose of painkillers in the hopes that I could avoid filling the prescription for morphine that was waiting for me at the pharmacy. This second day after round two was the first day that I lost large gaps of time and was unaware of what was going on around the house for most of the day. After three days, the bone pain began to ease, and I was finally able to get farther than a few steps from my bed. By the end of the week I could slowly, slowly make my way downstairs to sit on a chair outside for some fresh air. That weekend—five days after my infusion—was also the first time I encountered my next two recurring chemo side effects: heartburn and mouth peeling.

I am not a stranger to heartburn, having suffered with it essentially from the moment of conception until birth with both of my daughters. However, this experience was more intense, as the heartburn returned with the might of a rhinoceros. I'd wake up in the night feeling like my esophagus was about to fall out while also being on fire. The standard advice for heartburn sufferers—limit spicy or acidic foods, try over-the-counter meds—was useless because I had hardly eaten anything outside the beige colour spectrum in days, and the acid reflux medications I chewed like candy weren't taking the burning down by a single degree.

Next came the mouth peeling, which was a distraction from the heartburn, but one I could have done without. The inside of my mouth felt like I had eaten several party-sized bags of salt and vinegar chips against my will and that I'd eventually just swallowed the chips whole instead of even bothering with chewing. My gums hurt, my tongue hurt, all the way to the back of my throat hurt. The entirety of the digestive system contains rapidly dividing cells, so literally from the beginning to the end of my digestive tract was negatively affected by the chemotherapy. Everything I put in my mouth to eat or drink tasted wildly different from what it should have tasted like, and the mere sensation of food touching the top of my mouth was discomforting. Like the result of eating too many salt and vinegar chips, my mouth peeled as the chemotherapy I received attacked the rapidly dividing cells inside my mouth on the quest for cancer domination. The sensitivity that I experienced was simply the feeling of brand-new skin cells that are not yet toughened up by age and the friction of rough and bumpy foods. It happens all the time inside everyone's mouth, just not in every single place at once. After the initial hypersensitivity, I then developed sores on my tongue and along my gums that made it difficult to try and eat anything that did not have the viscosity of pudding.

I assumed chemotherapy would get harder and harder, but I was not prepared for the vast difference between the first two cycles. I couldn't imagine what the next cycle would bring if the devastation continued to intensify with every cycle that was to come.

CHAPTER FIFTEEN

Cycle three of chemotherapy was indeed worse than its predecessors. Once again, the chemotherapy was hitting harder and faster and I deeply regretted those thoughts of how easily I assumed I would "handle this chemo business" following my first treatment.

"Here come the ice pans," Scott said, rousing me from the cat nap I had drifted into after the second bag of antinausea medications had been hooked to my IV line. Having a port in my body made it significantly more comfortable to be attached to an IV for hours at a time as medications could be added and empty bags removed from the queue without me even noticing the nurse at my bedside. The additional highly valued benefit of having a port is that it diminished the possibility of Adriamycin escaping my veins on the journey around my body and causing blistering so severe that any organ or tissue it touched would essentially melt. My veins could have incurred dramatic damage after six cycles of this medication being administered through them, and that burden was removed once the port was available, since the port is fundamentally a gateway directly into my heart. The improvement is relative here.

"Wake me when The Red Devil arrives," I replied. "No, wait. Unplug me first so I can go to the bathroom."

After returning from my bathroom road trip, I dipped my hands into the freshly filled ice pans and dozed on and off for the hour it took to receive the Taxotere. It felt like Scott woke me moments later, but when I opened my eyes at the sound of his voice, the nurse was walking towards my bed holding the unmistakable UV-blocking bag that signalled the arrival of the demon.

"Do you become accustomed to the blatant insanity of what's required before you give me this med? I mean, you're in full protective gear while injecting that into my heart," I asked, half laughing and half in mourning.

"Yes, but also no," she laughed back. "This one is a particularly intense chemotherapy. They aren't called cytotoxins for nothing, I suppose. You might know this already, but certain chemotherapy meds work on cancer cells that are newly converted from healthy cells, some work on cells as they are about to divide, and others work on cells that have been at the centre of a carcinoma for a long time."

"She has a lot of library books on cancer at home," Scott informed the nurse.

"Guilty," I replied, raising my hands in surrender to the charge.

"I love it," she encouraged. "So you know that, for better or worse, Adriamycin is one of the only chemo medications that can effectively destroy a cancer cell at every single stage. It's not without added consequences though."

"Like melting skin," Scott added.

"I see she isn't the only one using those library books," the nurse replied.

"In short, I have a tissue-melting red demon being injected into a port feeding directly into my heart so that it can blaze through my entire body and eviscerate cancer cells at every stage of maturity, taking with it most of the cells from inside my mouth, esophagus, stomach lining, intestines, and colon along the way and leaving me with a bottomed-out white blood cell count," I summarized.

"This isn't your first time here," came her solemn reply. "You also know why it's called The Red Devil by now, I'm sure?" she queried. "It's not only because it's red before we administer it."

"It turns her output orange, then red," Scott answered.

"So, add the fact that after application of The Red Devil, it'll look like I'm pissing blood for a day. It might be a situation where the nickname is not an exaggeration," I whispered. On my road to hell, cancer had laid the road, but Adriamycin drove the car and severed the brakes.

The nurse laughed again and just nodded. She'd finished emptying the syringe of devil liquid and began my saline flush, then she headed back to the nurses' station. I needed to get half of that bag of saline into me before I could start on the cyclophosphamide, and hopefully the half hour it would take me to drain the IV bag would be exactly how long it took for the final chemotherapy medication to arrive from the pharmacy.

I was asleep again before the saline flush completed, and when I awoke I made the trek back to the bathroom to expel orange urine. When I returned, I had to take my oral antinausea medications while still in the chemotherapy unit—the first time my nausea had begun before I'd even left the Cancer Centre. The cyclophosphamide was hooked up shortly after, and I held on for dear life as the chemotherapy roller coaster crested the top of the ascent and I looked out over the free fall awaiting me on the other side.

Once home after the third cycle, I held no illusions that I would be back on my feet and participating in my life as usual within ten days. I knew to expect the crash to begin on the second day post-chemo due to the combination of my steroids ending and the administration of the injection that boosted my white blood cell count. I started taking the steroids the day before chemotherapy, then took a double dose the day of, and took a final dose on the evening of the day after chemotherapy. Therefore, the second day after chemotherapy was always the first day that I was not artificially inflated with steroids, and it was also the day that I'd inject myself with liquid bone pain. I knew that after day two I would be confined to bed until my body recovered from the collateral damage of TAC.

Appetite changes were another side effect I learned to expect by the third cycle of chemo. Coffee tasted abhorrent for about a week and a half afterwards and water carried the metallic taste caused by a mouth constantly peeling, so I would only drink lemonade or carbonated water. I'd stock the fridge during the weekend before my chemotherapy appointment knowing it would be all gone before the next cycle started. Conversely, I also expected to experience wild food cravings while on the upswing from chemotherapy treatments. Immediately after an infusion I could eat nearly nothing, mostly because I was asleep seventy-five per cent of the time, but also because most foods positively disgusted me. One day, perhaps a week and a half after the treatment, a switch would flip and I would become ravenous for some kind of food and I could never anticipate what specifically that food would be. During chemo recovery three, it was spinach and cherry tomatoes with peanut sauce on top.

It was also during recovery after my third cycle that I could not bear the fire emanating from my esophagus any longer. Central Pharmacy, located in the Cancer Centre, dispenses all the medication received as an in-patient—medications like the chemotherapy drugs and all the antinausea medications I received in the hospital—but they did not dispense medications that patients take at home. The pharmacy team in the Cancer Centre does, however, have the ability to write prescriptions for many of the medications a cancer patient needs while enduring the side effects of chemotherapy, so I called them to ask for help to deal with my heartburn.

As soon as I mentioned heartburn and how bad mine had become, the pharmacist kindly chastised me for not asking for help sooner. To her credit, she was much kinder to me than I deserved as she told me to knock it off and ask for help.

"It's our job, Ashleigh," she said, scolding me. "I am literally here to listen to any side effects you experience and help manage them so you can keep your chemotherapy on schedule and also live your life as much as is reasonable during recovery."

"I do know that. I honestly can't explain why I felt I had to endure this one side effect," I admitted. "The ranitidine that you prescribed back in September isn't lessening my discomfort an iota, and I am basically treating them like candy."

"That's helpful information. Have you been taking them every day or only once symptoms begin?" she asked.

"At first, I was taking them once I had active heartburn, but after a week or so I started taking them daily. Now I am taking them in the morning and evening every day and it isn't making a difference. The burning is waking me up at night sometimes, it's so bad."

"It sounds like it's time for the introduction of a proton pump inhibitor. We'll start it immediately and you'll take it daily for the remainder of your chemotherapy treatments," she said. There was a brief pause and I heard typing, then her focus returned to me on the phone.

"Do you know what a proton pump inhibitor is?" she asked.

"Not a clue, but it sounds futuristic," I admitted.

"Essentially, it's a medication that will reduce the production of acid in your stomach, which is what's causing the heartburn."

"Will I still be able to digest food?" I asked. I already knew her answer was not going to sway my desire from taking the medication, as I was in so much discomfort I would have happily shut down my entire digestive tract for some relief.

"A proton pump inhibitor does not stop all acid production, just reduces it. Less acid in your stomach means that hopefully what does get produced is just enough to digest food, leaving a minimal amount left in your stomach afterwards. This way, there will be less for your stomach muscles to toss around as you're grappling with the effects of chemotherapy." I have a sudden vision of a car accident that is unavoidable—it would be preferential to have fewer freely moving objects flying around inside the vehicle to collide with the passengers.

"You also aren't eating as much in the days immediately after chemotherapy anyway, right?"

"Yeah, that's true. I'm not eating much and what I am eating tends to be pretty bland," I confirmed.

"Exactly. So, less acid is not going to have a noticeable effect on your ability to digest, but it will hopefully have a positive effect on the heartburn," she said encouragingly. "Are you also experiencing acid reflux? Small amounts of regurgitation in your mouth at times?"

"I am," I said.

"Over time, acid reflux and heartburn can damage the esophagus, because it's designed to encounter food on the way down, not after it's been broken down and doused in stomach acid. Occasional vomiting doesn't cause damage because your esophagus can heal in the time between illness. Long-term reflux eliminates any recovery period, so the proton pump inhibitor will also give your esophagus a break to heal as well," she concluded.

"So, the density of rapidly dividing cells in my digestive system means everything in there is in turmoil every time I receive TAC. The proton pump inhibitor will reduce the acid my stomach produces and in turn reduce the heartburn and reflux." I want to understand the mechanism of the medications I take to help me rally the fortitude to take them; to carry on through the inevitable added side effects this medication will bring along with it.

"Simplistically, yes," she said. "You are understanding these complex subjects remarkably well."

"How do I take it? Is it a pill?'" I asked, wary of yet one more medication I had to ingest during the days of recovery.

"It is a pill," she immediately said.

Splendid, another pill.

I turned to look at the collection of prescription bottles already standing at attention beside my bed. The pharmacist's voice in my ear pulled me back from my despair at having to add yet another pill to my daily diet.

"You will take one every day from now until you finish chemotherapy, even on all the days when you're feeling fine. You'll also keep that ranitidine close at hand and add it in as an additional tool to combat the heartburn during the worst of the days you experience it," she finished.

"At this point, I'm taking seven different medications a day, sometimes multiple times a day, to counter the tidal wave of side effects chemo is causing, and I can't swallow pills," I reminded her.

"Oh, shoot. Right!" she immediately responded. "You're chewing most meds? And the time-release tablets are liquid instead?" I could hear the pharmacist's fingers typing at lightning speed over a keyboard as she asked me these questions.

"Yeah," I said, wearily. "I don't know if I can add another pill that I need to chew. I am already struggling to consume my meds to lessen nausea, bone pain, and anxiety, and I know I wouldn't prioritize this one when it comes to deciding which pills I'm able to keep down."

"Okay . . . ," she responded, hearing me but still searching for a solution in her database of medications. "The proton pump inhibitor comes in a dissolvable tablet!' she exclaimed. "You can simply lay it on the tongue, and it will disappear. I'll fax the prescription for this specific version to your regular pharmacy within the hour."

We hung up and I got ready to head to my pharmacy and pick up yet one more tablet to add to my menu of medications. The Cancer Centre pharmacist was true to her word, and the dissolvable proton pump inhibitor was waiting for me by the time I got in the lineup to collect it. At the front of the line, however, I learned that my insurance company was denying coverage. Of course, the dissolvable version of the proton pump inhibitor is the costliest to manufacture and, therefore, the pharmacy cost is higher than a more simplistic pill that is swallowed. My insurance company was only reimbursing twenty per cent of a $90 monthly prescription instead of the usual eighty per cent coverage because I was "choosing a specialized version" of the medication. It's particularly unconscionable how they made it sound like it was my choice to need it at all.

I paid the bill that day and took the medication that reduced my heartburn to a manageable level that same night. I needed a ranitidine or two in the days immediately after chemotherapy, but at least now the new medication worked and I could sleep without esophageal pain.

I went back and forth with my insurance company for months over the coverage of the proton pump inhibitor and they refused to budge—if I wished to take the medication in the dissolvable form, I had to demonstrate that I had exhausted all cheaper options before they would honour the eighty per cent prescription coverage that I received on other medications. Every engagement from myself, my medical oncologist, and the oncology pharmacists explaining that I physically could not force another pill inside my body went unacknowledged. Even the clarification that I would be on these inhibitors only temporarily and not as a long-term consumer was not heeded. In the end, I paid out $260 over four months for the medication, and I submitted a request for a review every single time I was denied full coverage when picking up my thirty-day supply. I never received a direct response to any of my subsequent requests for review of their denial.

CHAPTER SIXTEEN

"When's the MRI?" Scott asked as he entered our bedroom. He sat on the bed beside me as I struggled to pull my eyelids open to see him before he left for work. I was forty-eight hours out from my third cycle of chemo and this was the first day of the beginning of my crash into bone pain, heartburn, mouth peeling, and the general inability to keep my eyes open for longer than thirty minutes.

"Next week, I think?" was my soft reply. "Check the wall."

"Ah, yes, the command centre of our cancer space station," he replied, standing up to turn and examine the wall opposite the foot of our bed. "I assumed you'd have the date of the first scan committed to memory as soon as the appointment was given to you."

Shortly after my diagnosis with invasive cancer, the appointments really began to pile up. Diagnostic imaging to find the carcinoma, blood tests, medical oncology appointments, surgical oncology appointments, chemotherapy preparation and on and on. I needed a place to coalesce all the times and dates that I had to be at a particular place at a particular time but did not wish to turn the primary living spaces of our home into a three-dimensional day planner for cancer co-ordination. I drew out eight months of calendars on huge sheets of paper and taped them to the wall in our bedroom so we could sit on the bed and look at the weeks as they came up and know where I had to be, when, and for how long. It was also helpful to have a visualization of what weeks I would be receiving chemotherapy so we could all know that not much was going to happen in the week after. We would decline invitations to go basically anywhere during those seven days, as my immune system would be at its absolute worst, and I couldn't risk illness that would delay treatment.

After the calendars were put up and began to be filled in with commitments, we could also see the halfway mark of my six planned chemotherapy treatments. Once I'd finished three rounds of my TAC regime, there would be a bevy of diagnostic testing to ensure that the parts of my insides that I wanted to keep intact were holding up okay and that the parts I wanted to expel were showing signs of retreat.

"I don't even know what day of the week it is today. Next week is only a possibility to me right now," I managed to say.

"Fair," Scott replied. "You focus on recovery. I am just anxious to know if . . ." he trailed off.

"I know. Me too," I mumbled. "I think."

It was indisputable that things were happening to my carcinomas. The mass in my breast was at first getting softer, softer, and then noticeably smaller, smaller. Every time I saw an oncology professional who had a comparison point for my carcinoma from before I had begun chemotherapy, I would practically jump at them to get them to feel the change and confirm to me that it wasn't just in my head.

That upcoming MRI, though, would provide more than an opinion. It would provide an answer in the face of all the hope I placed in the spaces that the cancer seemed to be leaving vacant inside my breast. What if the hope was misplaced? The MRI results would not be debatable in the same way the changing external appearance and tactile differences that I had tracked over the course of the previous nine weeks could be debated. The MRI results were proof of concept of the application of chemotherapy, but what if they proved it to be unsuccessful?

"Go back to sleep," Scott said gently. "In case you're curious, your MRI isn't for another nine days," he reported.

"You're coming with me?" I asked in response.

"Of course."

"Grand," I replied and then gave in to exhaustion.

Pre-cancer, I would throw around the phrase "couldn't leave bed" when I was exceedingly sick; however, what I really meant was that I'd stayed in my PJs and sat in my bed binging Netflix between bathroom and kitchen visits and cat naps. It's never fun to be sick enough that every facet of life slows to a crawl, but in the days after chemotherapy treatment number three, I literally could not even sit in an upright position. I could not get from horizontal in bed to upright in the kitchen if my life had literally depended on it. Not only could I not watch Netflix, but I also couldn't even spell Netflix for the worst thirty-six-hour period after my third round of chemo. I became a slug, a comparison more insulting to slugs than to me in my post-chemo state.

Outside of my debilitating exhaustion and my eviscerated digestive system, the remainder of my body was also not demonstrating any sense of joy or relief at the possibility of a slowing cancer advancement. I had begun to have chest pains that were unrelated to the port since that was well healed, and I was afraid that the Adriamycin was messing around with something that I could not come back from. After I made it to the other side of the hardest days of recovery from chemo cycle three, I requested a phone call with my medical oncologist to discuss the chest pains

I was having and my fear that they were being caused by the Adriamycin.

My medical oncology team had been nothing but supportive of me. They'd laid out the facts of my diagnosis at each step of treatment and helped me weigh every option and side effect with patience and honesty. This conversation was no different on the part of the doctor I was speaking to; however, it was different when considering my own motivation during our conversation. Instead of seeking information during that call, I was negotiating. I wanted out from my mortal dependence on chemotherapy, but I did not want the regret that I knew I would carry if I made the choice to stop and ever, ever faced a cancer diagnosis again in the future. I wanted there to be some other reason why I had to stop repeatedly recovering from The Red Devil. I wanted there to be an unavoidable reason I could no longer follow the TAC regime, even though it was considered the most robust response to estrogen/progesterone-positive, HER2-negative breast cancer that science could produce. I wanted any future regret to be assuaged by the fact that if I continued with this line of treatment, my heart would be destroyed. You know you're in a bad place when you're wishing that your heart is exploding so you can stop taking the chemotherapy medications that are likely reducing your cancer.

My medical oncologist listened and told me that nothing that I was experiencing sounded like damage that Adriamycin could cause. To back this up, she had reviewed my most recent heart scans before returning my call to make sure everything looked as it should. After hearing that my heart was likely as okay as it could be at this stage, I went directly to the library books that I still had, and likely owed fines on by that point. I spent some time with those books and with online patient resources reminding myself how effective Adriamycin often proves to be. I could choose not to continue with the plan laid out ahead of me, but it would have to be my own choice and not a medical necessity. I doubled down on science and then, resigned, fully and wholly committed to going the distance with The Red Devil.

As if all this wasn't enough, days after this conversation with my medical oncologist, I began four weeks of menstruation of such a wildly unpredictable volume that an ultrasound was ordered to ensure the chemotherapy was not causing negative side effects within my uterus. The mystical black and white swirly images of the ultrasound did not reveal anything sinister happening and the bleeding stopped as abruptly as it began. That prolonged menstruation would be the final period of my life. At thirty-five years old, and having undergone three cycles of TAC chemotherapy, I was menopausal.

CHAPTER SEVENTEEN

Then, it was mid-September and finally MRI day. It was time to put the magnets where my monster was and get back in that MRI machine for a solid scientific assessment of how much less solid my cancer was. Into the industrial dryer full of magnets I went, table slid in, table slid out, dye added, table slid back in one final time. I was back in my own clothing and out of the hospital within an hour this time.

Days later, Scott and I were once again in an examination room inside a Cancer Centre clinic—me sitting on an examination table in a hospital gown, him holding the clothing I'd shed—as we waited for my medical oncologist. This time we knew what we were waiting for. There would be no surprise in learning results were available and there would be no misunderstanding when reading the technical words printed on the page.

This time, it was the most glorious news: Chemo! Was! Working!

By every measurable matrix, the carcinoma had been reduced: first by feel, now density and diameter. This revelation brought tears and laughter and joy as my belief of improvement was validated, then frustration and sadness that success at the halfway mark still meant I had half of the chemotherapy treatments left to receive and recover from.

It was only after I had scientific proof that the cancer was being eradicated that I realized that my breast felt different to the remainder of my body. Prior to beginning chemotherapy, my right breast was almost stationary on my chest. Now, with three cycles of chemo reducing the carcinoma interloper inside of it, my breast moved, hung, and squashed like a breast again and not like a baggie of cement attached to my chest. The change from healthy tissue to cancerous tissue was a slow, slow hardening that happened cell by cell. The change back was so swift and happened so dramatically, it seemed shocking that it took me so long to realize something had ever been wrong in the first place.

On the way home, Scott and I stopped at our regular pharmacy to pick up my litany of pre-chemo medications, as my next evisceration was only days away. The pharmacy in which I got all the medications I took at home was located inside a large department store and some of the staff had grown to recognize my face, both as a frequent customer picking up a $2,000 special-order injection and also as a walking reminder of mortality.

After picking up the precious medications, and as Scott and I walked out of the pharmacy section and past the main cash registers of the larger store, I saw a friend who worked there. Karen and I had not been close friends back when we'd first met in junior high; however, in the years since graduating high school we had crossed paths many times. Comically, we frequently ran into each other at pivotal times in our lives and eventually we would joke that something big must have happened to one of us recently whenever we saw each other. Two decades of consistent unplanned meetings had accumulated and developed into a genuine adult friendship.

Karen was aware of my medical diagnosis, and as soon as she saw me, she came right over to ask how things were going. I gleefully gave her a Cancer Muggle version of the report I'd just received and we literally danced in the aisle behind the cash registers in this enormous department store, both wiping tears of joy and catharsis from our eyes. As always, Karen asked how our kids were managing and greeted Scott by name. She proved that she hadn't simply nodded along during our conversations throughout the years, she had listened. Karen was the first person that I told with my own words and voice that I had the medical evidence to support hope that I may live.

Truthfully, the only reason I even showed up for the fourth cycle of chemo a few days later was because I had the knowledge that chemotherapy was working. Round three kicked my ass and it was unimaginable to believe that I had just as far left to travel ahead of me as was behind me. I didn't think I could go much lower than what I had just come back from. Undeniable medical imaging evidence that the regime was working was the fuel I needed to steel myself to either finish the six rounds of TAC or literally die trying to get there. Round four, here I come.

CHAPTER EIGHTEEN

I received chemotherapy every three weeks from July to November, but September was the only month during which I received chemotherapy twice. Recovery wise, it made no difference as there would still be three weeks between one treatment and the next. Emotionally, however, it was awful to see the word "CHEMOTHERAPY" written across two days in one month on the calendars taped to my bedroom wall. Financially, it also meant I had to pay for my pre-chemo medications twice in one month, and those costs added up fast.

Round four was the first time I truly had to drag myself into the building when chemotherapy day arrived. This is the deep mindfuck of receiving chemotherapy—as an adult, I had to participate in it happening. I had to pick up and pay for prescriptions knowing the agony they would cause me after I took them, and then get in my vehicle to go to appointments that would cause me even more distress in the days following. I had to register and sit in the waiting room while trying to maintain calm. I had to sit on a hospital bed for seven hours watching an insidious medical marvel enter my body knowing very well what it would do to me afterwards, and I had to not rip the lines from my port and run from the building. The necessity of having to sit next to an IV tree and watch the medications slowly, slowly be administered knowing full well what was going to happen when I got home is a form of psychological torture.

During this fourth round of torture a friend of mine, also named Ashleigh, came to visit with me while I was in the chemotherapy unit. She and I had gone to high school together nearly twenty years previously. By the violent and random hand of fate, we were now both battling breast cancer. I'd heard about her diagnosis the week after I'd had my first ultrasound falsely telling me that I was not to share this road with her. Now, here I was, just a few steps behind Ashleigh on a similar path. There is something about friendships forged in the fire of trauma—they're immediately intense and intimate. I didn't often talk specifics about a lot of my cancer experiences with my friends, but that wasn't a sign of a deficiency in our relationships. I know that many of my pre-cancer friends would have taken my call day or night if I needed to unload. It's the learning curve that makes that an emotional impossibility. I could say to Ashleigh as she was sitting on my hospital bed that the ice didn't feel particularly cold this cycle and she understood. I could tell her that I had a MUGA—multigated acquisition—scan coming up and she would know that the results would update me on the condition of my heart, and she'd also know exactly what it felt like to lie in the machine for that test—she had likely lain on a similar narrow bed recently for one scan or another, maybe even the exact same one. Again, any of my friends would listen to these experiences and allow me to unload, but as a former Cancer Muggle myself, I knew just how much they did not know and also the depth of what I could never accurately convey to them. It is in the unspoken understanding, in that lack of need to offer definitions and explanations, that patients of any demographic find solace in each other.

I had reached out to Ashleigh before I started chemotherapy and, through that forge of trauma, we had created a new friendship. Up until that point, however, it had been growing only through texting. We had never connected in person because of the hectic nature of appointments and the necessity for long periods of recovery that an active cancer patient has to manage, coupled with the fact that we both had young children who needed 100 per cent of us as soon as we were able to be present for them. We'd texted the morning of my chemotherapy appointment and discovered that we would both be at the Cancer Centre at the same time, and she told me she would come over to the chemotherapy unit after her appointment.

It was around mid-day when Ashleigh came in and sat on the bed beside me to share a few hugs and a bevy of tears. We cried for ourselves, and we cried for each other. She knew the nurses just like I did and several of them came over to say hello and laugh about how "of course the two Ashleighs know each other!" Being a young adult with cancer is a club with few members, so when both of us were there together it was noteworthy.

Ashleigh's breast cancer was a different type than mine, in fact it was among the most aggressive breast cancers that can be found in women under forty, and she had initially received a different chemo cocktail than I had. Her cancer was so aggressive in speed and scope that she had begun chemotherapy when she was pregnant with her youngest kid. I cannot begin to imagine the response a young, bald adult who was also pregnant would garner when walking into the Cancer Centre. I cannot begin to imagine the agonizing decisions placed at Ashleigh's feet when facing the despair of a diagnosis of aggressive breast cancer while simultaneously feeling the joy of life growing inside you. By the time she and I connected on the battleground of cancer, Ashleigh's breast cancer had progressed to stage 4 and she had a healthy baby at home. Where I got to stand

and joyfully yell "fuck yeah!" when I heard that my cancer had paused at stage 3, she would have had a diametrically opposite reaction, perhaps best expressed with a "fuck no!" when hearing that she had metastatic cancer in her lungs and, later, brain as well. This is yet another psychological torture of cancer—the random, unpredictable, shit luck that determined that my fight was going to be hard and her fight infinitely harder.

During our chat, Ashleigh told me about her recent trip to another province to participate in a clinical trial. When a new potential treatment is considered, it is sometimes refined with volunteer patients who join clinical trials to try out a new regime of medications, surgeries, or treatment processes in the hopes that the researchers have hit upon a miracle. It is often patients with cancers that have thwarted all known treatment protocols who are participating in these clinical trials. When all other treatments are exhausted and yet the cancer soldiers onward, many people are willing to try anything to slow its advancement. Refinements of approach to treatment, and sometimes discoveries of new medications that could save countless lives impacted by a cancer diagnosis, are perfected through these clinical trials, and the participants are most often volunteers who are in the process of losing their lives to the disease. This contribution—this sacrifice—is beautiful and also heartbreaking. While I am sure that extending her life was the primary objective of my friend's participation in the trial that she had just returned from, I would not be at all surprised if contributing to the advancement of cancer treatments was a small part of her motivation.

We cried again as Ashleigh told me that she was discharged from the trial because the regime being tested was not showing any signs of reducing her breast cancer. In addition to sharing a high school class, a first name, and a cancer diagnosis, Ashleigh and I shared the same medical oncologist, and she had just come from an appointment with our doctor where they had discussed palliative chemotherapy and radiation therapy. In what might be the heaviest conversation I have ever had with anyone besides my husband, she and I sat on the hospital bed while I received chemotherapy and we talked about death. We held hands and talked about being scared and angry and tired. We spent less than an hour in each other's company that afternoon, but we continued to text updates and support along with promises to get back together after my next chemotherapy recovery, after surgery, or after she settled into radiation therapy. We continued to text each other with absolutely no expectation of a reply because we both understood that the unpredictable life of a cancer patient could mean that a text arrived when one of us was physically unable to read it or respond. A friendship forged in trauma carries no expectations and yet can be among the most supportive in its understanding of the crisis at hand.

CHAPTER NINETEEN

By the time I arrived at the Cancer Centre for the fifth round of chemotherapy, I was an expert. I had my prescriptions filled days beforehand, I had taken every one of the doses of steroids that came before receiving TAC, my needle disposal box was ready to receive a syringe after it had been emptied of all the white-blood-cell-producing medication, and the sheets on my bed were freshly changed. I'd made a duffle bag months before that accompanied me to every Cancer Centre appointment that I had embroidered with a personal mantra of #fuckcancer and inside it were snacks, a cellphone charger, mints to cover the salty taste I'd get in my mouth when saline solution was pushed through my port, and a change of clothing in case whatever I'd chosen to wear that day was incompatible with whatever side effects I experienced during that particular round of chemo. As a seasoned chemotherapy recipient, I knew it was unlikely I would make it past lunchtime before the weight of the medications would drag me down, so I requested a bed to rest in for the day instead of a reclining chair.

I was in that bed after lunch when a man walked into the chemotherapy unit with the stride of someone that had been there many times before. He was clearly not a doctor or nurse as he was dressed in jeans, boots, and a jacket, so he had to be either a patient or there with someone as accustomed to the chemotherapy unit as I was. Then he stopped beside my bed.

"Hey... wait, no," he fumbled as he appeared to offer a greeting to me before noticing Scott sitting in the chair on the other side of my bed.

"Hey! Over here!" called a voice from the corner directly across from me.

Scott, the man, and I all looked over to see a woman sitting in a reclining chair and hooked to an IV smiling broadly at the trio of us. She was bald, she was young, and she looked strikingly like me. Her name was Deanne, and I am confident she has never let her partner forget the day he mistook me for her when entering the chemotherapy unit during her treatment for breast cancer.

As evidenced by my well-packed bag and the knowing stride of Deanne's partner, we were both veterans of chemotherapy on the day we met. We were both aware that while we likely had a lot in common as the youngsters in the unit, it would be difficult to begin a friendship while literally receiving treatments. My TAC medications attacked both healthy and cancerous cells with equal intensity and, while my healthy cells would regenerate briefly in the three weeks between cycles, there were now fewer cancer cells to absorb the attention of the chemotherapy medications. By the time I sat across from Deanne in the chemotherapy unit for cycle number five, my ratio of cancer cells to healthy cells had been dramatically reduced, yet the volume of the TAC regime remained the same. The effects of chemotherapy on the healthy portions of my body continued to be felt earlier and earlier each cycle, until I showed up already feeling like a slug before the needle even pierced the skin above my port. Fundamentally, the worse I felt, the worse Deanne felt, the closer we both were to the end of chemotherapy treatments. We exchanged pleasantries that day and also phone numbers so that we could connect again in the days after when we'd become human once more.

I would have given anything to experience the recovery I had after cycle three when I thought I was at the lowest of the low, because round five was my rock-bottom on the chemotherapy roller coaster. After round five, it took a full week before I could get out of bed in the morning and not need to sleep at least once throughout the day. The sores in my mouth became the worst those beasts had ever been, both in quantity and discomfort. My heartburn returned and, while it was beaten back with ranitidine, I had not had to take the extra medication for as many consecutive days since starting on the proton pump inhibitor. Food did not regain its flavour and I did not crave any specific things to eat because I just did not want to eat anything. I did not recover in any significant sense of the word between chemo cycles five and six, entangling the final six weeks of my chemotherapy treatments into one long nightmare.

The singular, shining bright memory that I have from those six weeks is of Halloween. Somehow, for over an hour, I managed to rally the strength to walk around my neighbourhood with my two kids and my best friend while wearing Hogwarts cloaks and waving magic wands. The climate in Newfoundland can be unpredictable at the best of times and there have been many Halloween adventures throughout the years that necessitated snowsuits; however, this night was clear, cool, and perfectly fall as if nature had rallied along with me for that brief moment. Scott was dressed head to toe as a Gryffindor student and I was dressed as a Ravenclaw student as we crossed the front yards of the houses up and down our street, watching our two kids dressed as Harry Potter and Hermione Granger gleefully collecting candy. It is yet another memory that Scott and my kids have given me that I will cherish for the remainder of my life. After about an hour of slowly walking, and shortly after the sun had set, I was hit with a wave of exhaustion and needed to head home. After accompanying me back home, Scott and my girls continued on their quest for candy acquisition while I went straight to bed.

Chemotherapy round six was comparatively a touch easier on me than round five had been. Perhaps it was because I knew that whatever the height of the mountain I had to climb back up, once I reached the top I would not be plummeting back down again in three weeks. At least not because of Taxotere, Adriamycin, and cyclophosphamide, anyway.

November 4th is the anniversary of mine and Scott's first date. I was nineteen at that time and Scott was twenty-one. Sixteen years and one day later, I received my final round of TAC chemotherapy; I was thirty-five and Scott was thirty-seven.

"I bet you never envisioned we'd ever be sitting here under these circumstances when we went on that first date," I said.

"I think I'd have believed I'd make it to Mars before I'd considered cancer would be in our lives before forty," he countered.

I fell asleep before I could adequately reply.

PART THREE

surgery

Just because someone carries it well,
it doesn't mean it isn't heavy.

CHAPTER TWENTY

From the first moment that my general practitioner nodded his head to confirm that I did have breast cancer, I knew that I was going to have a mastectomy. When you are in a horrid situation, sometimes your correct course of action lights up for you with the candlepower of a landing strip and you know exactly what you'll do. I tried to negotiate my way out of finishing six rounds of TAC, and I struggled to make decisions around other surgeries that would be optioned to me. In contrast, every single time the surgical question was asked, I always knew I would be having a surgery that fully removed my breast: a mastectomy. I was also adamant that not just the cancerous breast was going to be excised, but both would be removed—a bilateral surgery (if one breast is removed it is called a unilateral mastectomy; however, some survivors who have opted for a unilateral surgery prefer to call themselves "unicorns").

I was given two surgical options: a mastectomy or a lumpectomy. A mastectomy is the total removal of all mammary tissue on the chest, including ducts, glands, and nipple. A lumpectomy is a surgery that aims to remove the identified mass in a breast along with a margin of additional tissue around the site while leaving the unaffected components of the breast intact. There is a page at the very beginning of my cancer journal where I attempted to make a Pros/Cons list of having a mastectomy versus a lumpectomy. There's nothing written on that page because every time I opened the notebook and tried to add anything to any of the four columns, all I could think about was laying on my bed the morning that I got the first urgent call to see my general practitioner. All I could sense was the echo of the feeling of knowing that I had cancer. The morning when I pre-gave up is all I could feel, smell, or taste whenever I tried to consider any surgical path outside of full breast removal. There was never any collection of pros for lumpectomy or cons for mastectomy that would outweigh the pro of never having to relive those minutes again. My logic was that it would be unlikely that I would be diagnosed with a new breast cancer if I no longer had any breasts at all.

The second question I had to answer was whether I intended to have reconstructive surgery after my mastectomy. There are a multitude of post-mastectomy procedures possible for those battling breast cancer who wish to live with breasts after their treatment has been completed. The one option that not one person independently brought up to me was to choose to live flat, or breastless, after a bilateral or unilateral mastectomy. I often brought up this option as something I was strongly considering when asked what my surgical preferences were, and most of the time the response I got was some iteration of "Well, you have lots of time to decide." A reply that I found condescending and presumptuous because the unspoken implication was that I had time to change my mind and have a reconstruction. Perhaps I *had* decided. No one ever suggested I had time to change my mind and live flat if I suggested I might have reconstruction in the future.

I unequivocally and enthusiastically support every choice that a person battling cancer makes regarding their body after a mastectomy. Immediate reconstruction, later reconstruction, lumpectomy, unilateral mastectomy . . . they're all valid choices because it's an individual choice. As long as the person with cancer is supported to make the choice that is right for them in relation to their own cancer, and is not pushed towards a surgical procedure that does not fit their goals for life after cancer, then the choice they make is the correct one. Additionally, plenty of people choose one path and decide later that they'd prefer to either remove their implants or have prosthetic surgery after being flat, and those decisions do not invalidate the person's initial choice. I advocate strongly for those working within cancer care to be more encouraging of breast cancer patients who choose to live flat after surgery for the simple fact that it is an option as valid as choosing prosthesis implantation in the months or years after a mastectomy, and patients need to hear and see that as an equally valid possibility.

I considered most options for reconstruction as I was going through chemotherapy, ultimately always deciding that if I did not feel strongly about prosthesis or tissue reconstruction as part of my post-cancer life at that moment, then I should probably not make a final decision yet. As I had done countless times before in my life when I did not know what course of action I should take, I sought out resources to fill in the gaps in my understanding. I went to the library and checked out every book I could find on breast cancer, focusing this time on resources that discussed life after treatment. After that, I looked up the medical journals that the books referenced whenever I wanted to know more. Once I began to read up on the process of receiving silicone breast implants, the entries in the "Cons" column of my personal Pros/Cons list got longer and also heavier.

At thirty-six years old, it was next to impossible for me to have silicone implants that would remain intact for the remainder of my life if I lived for multiple decades after cancer, because breast implants break down over time. The process of expanding my chest cavity and skin to accommodate breast prostheses takes time and would be uncomfortable at the best of times, plus any reconstruction I underwent would result in breast mounds that either did not have nipples at all or would have entirely artificial nipples with no sensation that would have to be tattooed to resemble the pigment of a human nipple. It would also be impossible for any option to be the exact same size and shape that my original parts had been. So, would reconstruction feel like my own breasts? Certainly nothing would mimic the same sensations of the set I was removing. If the reconstruction options available to me would not functionally replace any features of the breasts that I would lose in surgery, then what was my personal motivation for having reconstruction?

"'I spent so many hours breastfeeding," I told Becca on the phone one evening. "Breastfeeding feels like it was such a foundational aspect of my life as a mother, especially in the earliest days with both. Now I feel like I hate my breasts. I feel betrayed by them for allowing cancer in."

After a pause, Becca replied simply, "That's a complicated relationship to have with your own breasts."

I've thought about that statement countless times since.

My final TAC regime was administered on November 5th, 2019, after which I had to recover from the effects of the medications for a sixth and final time. Once again, it was a week before I was able to reliably stay awake all day, so it was mid-November before I was able to dedicate any brain space towards preparations for major surgery. The plan was for my bilateral mastectomy to happen swiftly after completing chemotherapy, since there was little purpose in suffering through all those weeks of bone pain, mouth sores, and an overall absence from my own life only to allow any cancer that remained to mount an unchecked resurgence after the final onslaught was administered. I needed a week to recover mentally and physically from chemotherapy and then a few more weeks for my white blood cell count to rebound to a level appropriate for my body to heal from the trauma of surgery, so I expected to get a call for a surgery date sometime in late November or early December.

On November 19th, my oncology surgeon's office called me to inform me that my bilateral mastectomy would be happening on the morning of November 28th.

After finishing the brief call, I immediately entered planning mode.

Just over a week to fill the freezer with food.

Just over a week to pull together a hospital bag containing clothing suitable for my post-surgery body, all my medications, and a robust selection of snacks to ensure I was not solely reliant on hospital meals.

Just over a week until I would never need to wear a bra again.

CHAPTER TWENTY-ONE

"Since the cancer in my breast is responding to chemotherapy, does that mean the cancer in my lymph nodes is as well?" I asked. It was the one question that had kept me awake at night even more than the steroids had over the course of my five months of chemotherapy.

"The assumption is that it is, right?" Scott replied, sounding equally as unsure of the answer. "Because it's the same cancer, so the same chemo should be effective."

"But, how do I know for sure?" I wondered as we sat on our couch. It was the night before my final appointment with my surgeon before my mastectomy.

At every appointment I had had during the weeks of chemotherapy, my medical oncologist would perform a physical exam of my breast and lymph nodes. Unlike the carcinoma in my breast that could practically be seen shrinking from one evening meal compared to breakfast the next day, whatever was going on in my lymph nodes remained a mystery.

I carried the burning question that the lymph nodes posed with me when I went to the appointment the next afternoon.

"I can see, I can feel the difference in my breast over the course of chemotherapy treatments. Plus, the MRI was pretty definitive. Chemotherapy is having a positive effect on the carcinoma," I stated, while sitting in the oncology surgeon's office. "How do you know if it's working as effectively on the cancer cells that made it to my nodes? Do we assume it is and leave the nodes? Or do we assume it isn't and take them all just in case?"

"Both of those are options," he replied. "There is a strong case to be made for the efficacy of your chemotherapy regime against those cancer cells as well. They originated in the carcinoma in the breast tissue and chemo has been effective at reducing growth there."

Point for Scott on that one.

"That would mean I can keep my lymph nodes?" I asked, and yet I sighed. "I feel like you are about to make a compelling argument for the opposite." Nothing about cancer is ever simple, ever straightforward, ever easy.

"Well, we know without a doubt that cancer did spread locally to your axillary nodes. The hope is that your chemotherapy regime destroyed the cancer cells that existed anywhere else just as effectively, but there is only one way to be absolutely certain," he stated.

"Removing them and looking at the pathology," I finished, already feeling the weight of yet another decision with neither a right nor a wrong option.

"That's correct; however, there is another option to consider. Instead of leaving all the lymph nodes and hoping chemotherapy was effective at eliminating all the cancer present or removing all the lymph nodes just in case it wasn't, you can have a sentinel node biopsy during your mastectomy," the surgeon said. "A sentinel node biopsy would involve having dye injected into your breast tissue—'"

"'More dye! What colour this time?" I asked, my voice dripping in sarcasm.

"Blue, actually," he replied with a straight face.

"That's new."

"This time," he continued, "it's injected into the breast tissue a few hours prior to your surgery so that the nodes have time to pick it up and pass the dye along the lymph node chain under your arm. Your surgery team will identify the first nodes in the chain based on which ones have absorbed the blue dye, and then we'd remove only the first half dozen instead of all of them."

"Then those can be looked at under the microscope," I concluded.

"Precisely. Those first few nodes that are removed can be examined to determine if any cancer cells remain. If only one or two nodes contain cancer cells or, even better, if none do, then it is reasonable to assume that there isn't cancer in any other nodes farther along the chain," he explained.

It's pass-the-parcel, only cancer.

"Cancer originated in the breast, so if we find a long sequence of lymph nodes leading away from the breast that are free of cancer, it becomes exceedingly unlikely that there would be any found at the opposite end of that sequence," he concluded.

"How many nodes are in there?" I asked, always interested in an otherwise useless fact about the body.

"Typically, eighteen to twenty-four in each axillary, but thirty or more is possible. Less than ten can occur as well. It really varies from body to body," he answered.

"So, a sentinel node biopsy leaves the possibility of retaining some lymph nodes while also providing some assurance of the distance that the cancer may still be stretching within that node chain." I paused here for disagreement and received none. "It sounds as if it's the best of both scenarios?" I asked, sure there would be a catch even with this course of treatment.

"I don't disagree that it combines positive aspects of both courses of action. I will clarify, however, that a sentinel node biopsy also includes some negatives as well."

Knew it.

"Yes, having a sentinel node biopsy instead of removing all of your nodes means you would keep lymphatic functionality on your right side. Your remaining lymphatic system will not be as effective as it was prior to removing the sentinel nodes. Your body is accustomed to having all the nodes that are there now and we will be removing some of that grouping. It may have an effect on the success of the remaining nodes to perform their role in draining lymph fluid, especially if you happen to be one of the people that has fewer nodes to begin with. I would consider the chances low that you'd notice that impact, but it is possible."

"That's the downside of removing just the sentinel nodes if they come back without any cancer, right? I'd have unnecessarily compromised my lymphatic system. What's the downside if they all come back with cancer in them?" I immediately asked.

"Then we have another decision to make. Should we go back in again for a second surgery and remove all the lymph nodes?" he replied. "That would mean that you'd be having two surgeries, two recovery periods. Twice as much exposure to the risks that come with any surgical experience," he paused here to allow me to have time to consider this branch of the surgical decision tree ahead of me.

"Or do we leave the nodes, knowing there was residual cancer in some, and monitor the area closely for evidence of cancer regrowth," he concluded. "I'm confident you can foresee the potential downside to that decision."

"Yeah, I see it," I said, deeply in thought. I was calculating the columns of pros and cons for each surgical decision as well as their unique sub-decisions as I sat on the exam table. At this point in my cancer patient career, I had a master's degree in medical procedure accounting.

"Can you see the cancer when the nodes are removed?" I asked. "In real time, there in the operating room?"

"Excellent question. Yes, and also no," he hedged. "We will take a look at the nodes under a microscope during the surgery. If there are any significant signs of cancer among the majority of them, I would like to get your permission in advance to remove all the nodes at that time."

"Of course," I immediately replied.

"However, the report that will be the deciding factor comes from pathology. They will thinly slice the nodes so that each layer can be examined. There could be microscopic cancer cells inside a node small enough that they will not be visible with the view we can access during surgery."

"Will that happen with my breast too? The slicing," I asked with curiosity. I'm imagining a deli meat slicer in the corner of the pathology lab creating thin slices of my removed body parts.

"Yes. The breast with cancer and also the one without."

"Wild."

"Ashleigh, we will also examine the tissue on your chest wall," he continued, wrenching my thoughts away from the pathology meat slicer and back to the reality of my own upcoming butchering.

"If any suspicious cell behaviour is noted after the removal of your breast tissue, we will need your preapproval to further excise any tissue presenting visually with markers of cancer growth. You already know that cancer can invade inward and infiltrate the chest musculature as it expands outward from a breast, so we will be looking for evidence of invasive movement on the chest wall as well," he explained.

"Whatever needs to go, goes. Do it," I replied, my confident tone more a reflection of my belief in the medical team around me than a belief in my ability to face news of more cancer after I awoke from surgery.

"Do the sentinel node biopsy. I'll deal with the outcome of cancer still being there if it comes to that," I said. Then I signed all the necessary paperwork and left the Cancer Centre behind me once again.

Bean, me, Scott and Ava the day before Scott shaved my head in preparation for chemotherapy.

Me with Scott at a beach near our home after recovery from my second round of chemotherapy.

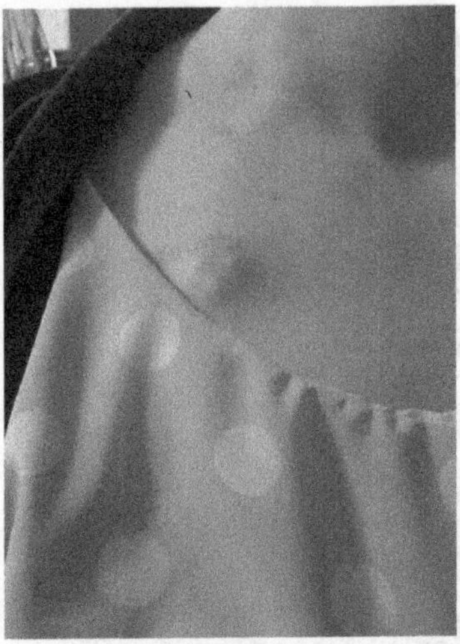 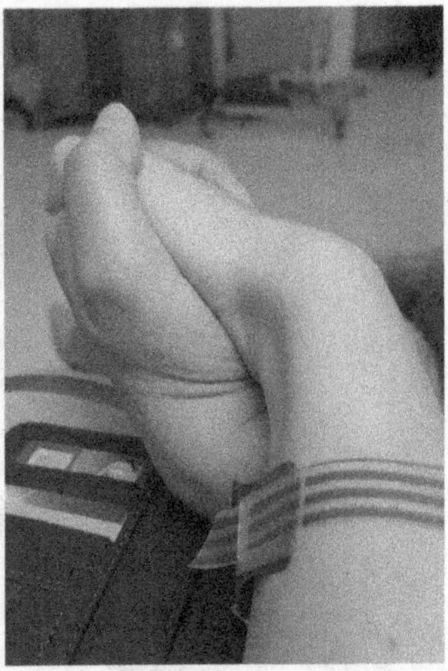

LEFT: *The port under the skin below my clavicle. The three bumps help to locate the perfect access point for a needle.*

RIGHT: *Becca holding my hand as chemotherapy started to tire me out. She flew halfway across the country to accompany me as I received my second round of chemotherapy.*

Me with Deanne on the day her partner mistook me for her in the chemotherapy unit.

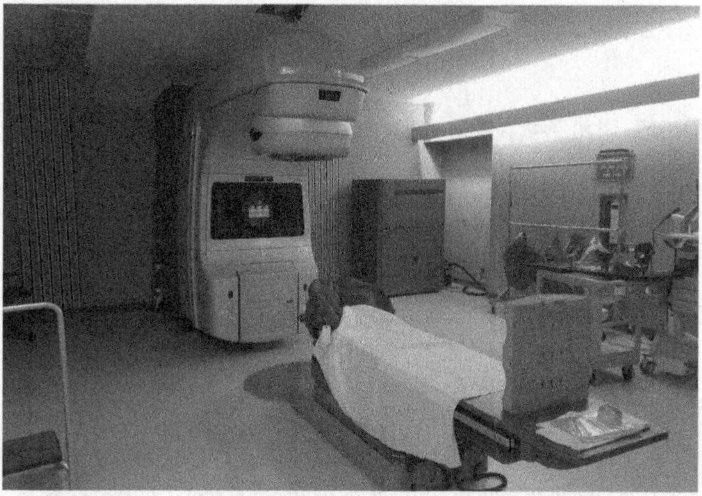

The radiation therapy machine that I lay under every day for twenty-five days of treatments.

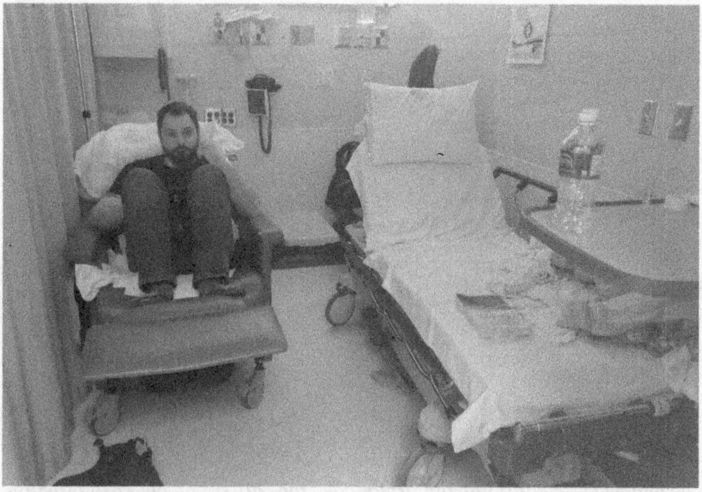

My gurney and Scott's "bed" during our two days of entrapment at the hospital during Snowmageddon. On the other side of the curtain on the left, another patient and their support person slept. Across from us, two more patients in similarly small and discomforting set-ups spent the days waiting out the storm.

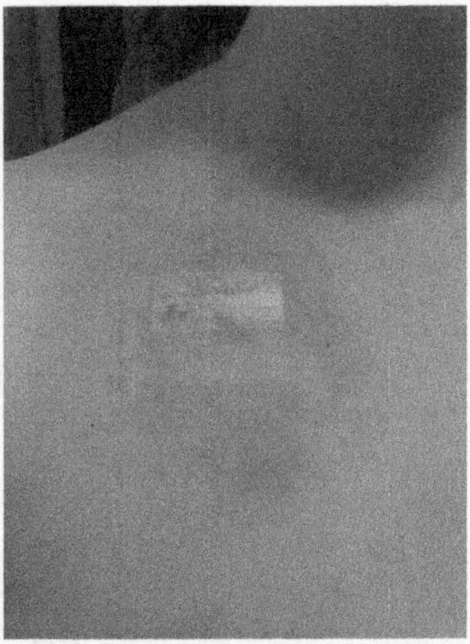

LEFT: On the one-year anniversary of my diagnosis of cancer, I flew a kite.
RIGHT: My port site after the removal of the device. The device was removed through the original incision site so the explant procedure did not add another scar to my chest.

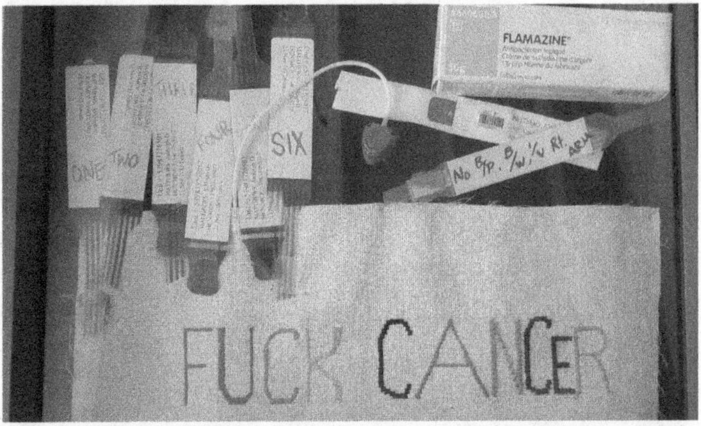

A shadowbox containing the armbands from all six of my chemotherapy treatments, the port that was inside my chest for over eight months, the armbands from each of my surgeries, and the packaging from a box of Flamazine®. The subversive embroidery was given to me by my friend Miranda.

CHAPTER TWENTY-TWO

Six days before my surgery, I arrived at the general hospital for my pre-admission appointment. First, I met with a nurse to discuss my medical history and what to expect during recovery for my specific surgery, then a physiotherapist, lastly an anesthesiologist. I already knew that I was going to be admitted after the surgery, so I also filled out all the paperwork for a planned hospital stay once the surgery was complete. I had blood work done to ensure my white blood cell count had rebounded sufficiently. The physiotherapist showed me the exercises that would expedite the timeline of regaining strength in my arms and upper body. The anesthesiologist assessed my lung health and overall fitness for the surgery I was preparing for. I finished pre-admission, and was cleared for surgery after five hours in the hospital on November 22nd, 2019, one day after my thirty-sixth birthday.

The night before my bilateral mastectomy was emotional for everyone in my family, yet for different reasons for each person. My youngest daughter, Bean, was very concerned about how she would get to sleep the following night since she knew that I definitely wouldn't be there at bedtime. My oldest daughter was trying very hard to be strong and brave for her little sister but was also holding on to a lot of feelings about not seeing me for at least twenty-four hours. My husband was fastening his superhero cape once again and juggling the needs of me and both of our kids while also processing his own fears about what would happen in our life if my surgery did not go as we hoped. I insisted on normalcy during the evening and throughout bedtime of the night before so that my kids wouldn't feel as afraid or anxious, and then promptly lost my composure and dissolved into a weepy puddle of tears and fears once they were both asleep. All in all, we looked and felt as one would expect a close family to look and feel knowing they would be facing a life-altering event the next day.

My in-laws, Wanda and Ron, came to stay with us the afternoon before my operation so that they could be settled with the kids well in advance of my leaving the following morning. Scott needed to spend the entire day at the hospital without worrying about how the kids were faring, and the best way to ensure that could happen would be to have them stay in their own home with their grandma. Scott spent the morning with me in the pre-op unit, and once I headed to the operating room, he spent the remainder of the day drinking bitter coffee and making small talk with his father and both of my parents in the hospital cafeteria.

Clad only in two thin and drafty hospital gowns, without any underwear on, sitting in the waiting area just before being escorted to the operating room was particularly disorienting because my glasses were back with my other personal items. Without them, I cannot see anyone well enough to identify them until they are literally directly in front of my face. My own surgeon walked past me while I was sitting on a gurney waiting for the final checks of the operating room to be completed, and I only knew it was him because I saw a blurry shape stop abruptly and circle back towards me. When he came over to check on me, I did feel some of my monumental anxiety ebb. That is not to suggest that I was suddenly calm and collected—far from it—but as soon as he stopped to check in with me, I was reminded exactly why I was proceeding with this major surgery and how much I trusted the professional opinions and skills of all the oncologists taking care of me. It's so important that the people surrounding a patient are trustworthy professionals because it takes a significant amount of emotional weight from the patient when the people giving advice on how to save their life are skilled enough to carry that emotional weight for them.

After a brief introduction to half a dozen medical staff who would be present in the room for my surgery, none of whom I could identify immediately afterwards because of my lack of glasses, I walked with a nurse down a short corridor and into a room that could never be mistaken for anything other than a surgical suite. When I was giving birth to Ava, I had been moved to an operating room because she was breech, and I had thought that operating room was the most surgical-looking a room could be; however, the room I had just entered made the previous operating room seem like a janitorial closet in comparison.

There were gigantic lights on the ceiling, a narrow bed in the centre, and more monitors, screens, and machines than in a cinematic rendering of a NASA launch. There were also half a dozen people already in the room checking off lists and pushing around small trays of tools. As I entered the operating room just a few steps behind the nurse, I saw smiles on all the faces close enough for me to make out their facial features. They weren't oh-she's-so-young-and-has-cancer smiles, but rather the smiles of people seeing a friend that they'd been waiting on. The willingness of these professionals to pause and say hello to me, to get me a warm blanket, to lean over me and reintroduce themselves, is something I will never forget.

Prior to the start of the surgery, a surgical resident came to stand at my side and asked for my name and for me to briefly explain what I understood was going to happen during the surgery. Just as I was saying the words "bilateral mastectomy with sentinel node biopsy," my oncology surgeon came into the room. Things were starting to feel imminent now. I was laying on the narrow table, and I had confirmed that I was the right person in the right room with the right team around me. This was truly happening, and that's when I started to cry. Grief for all that I had already lost and was about to lose poured from my body. Relief that the physical part of my body that had harboured my potential death would no longer be a part of me at the end of this day. Fear that this might be the last day for me, and thus this moment might be my last moment of conscious knowledge, because nothing is guaranteed during surgery. The surgical resident who was standing by my side put a comforting hand on my arm and continued to look directly into my teary eyes.

"Do you have any questions before we start your sedation, Ashleigh?" she asked, her voice calm and her demeanour patient. This surgeon knew my name without needing to look at my chart.

"Yes. I need someone, anyone—but preferably everyone—to salute my breast after it's removed from my body. After all the grief, anger, and fear it has put me through, it deserves a proper send off," I said as I mimicked waving goodbye with both my hands but with only my middle fingers extended.

"I understand that you're all medical professionals, but I just need to believe that it can happen," I rushed to explain before any of the people in the room could decline my request.

"It can," replied the surgical resident, as I saw several other members of the surgical team nodding in agreement. My tears could not be stopped.

A silicone mask was placed over my face and one of the nurses standing beside me bent down to tell me to start taking deeper breaths whenever I was ready. I filled my lungs as deeply and quickly as my physiology would allow so I could escape the moment of grief, relief, and fear and get on with the next part. I had contemplated the mastectomy elephant enough as a whole and it was about time for me to take the next bite.

CHAPTER TWENTY-THREE

I woke up just a moment later to the sound of a female voice kindly but firmly saying "Ash-le-eee, it's time to waaaake up."

I opened my eyes and realized that my view had changed from the one I had closed my eyes to a few seconds ago, and then I closed my eyes again. I heard the same voice call my name and before I opened my eyes this time I remembered where I was and why.

I opened my eyes again and even though there was no one in front of me I started repeating, "Is it done? Is it done?" I kept saying this even as my eyelids dropped closed once more.

For the third time, I heard my name being spoken near me in a low, yet persistent tone. When I opened my eyes again, I turned my head to see a nurse beside me.

"Is it done?" I asked one more time.

"Yes," she replied. "You're out of surgery now. It's all done."

Prior to surgery, I had been advised that deep breathing as soon as possible after waking from anesthesia would help me come around to consciousness quicker, so I tried to take a big, deep breath and that's when I realized that my chest was tightly bound. It was indeed done.

Slowly, slowly I became more and more wakeful. Eventually, a nurse was beside me once again, this time asking if I knew that I was being admitted tonight. I acknowledged with a head nod that I did know and immediately felt deeply nauseous. I assumed it to be a side effect of the disorientating experience of waking up from surgery in a different time and place, but I also simultaneously thought that it was peculiar that she'd phrased her question as "being admitted tonight" since it was at most early afternoon when she asked.

Heavily bandaged, and laying on my back wrapped in blankets on a gurney, the trek to my room was mostly a series of quickly moving ceiling tiles, an elevator ride, and several corridors filled with partially opened hospital room doors in front of low voices.

I had last seen Scott when I walked out of the pre-op room wearing paper slippers and two hospital gowns at ten o'clock that morning. I had, of course, flashed him one last time as I was changing into those gowns. As my gurney was swung into the room I'd be sleeping in that night and parked beside the stationary hospital bed that I was to be transferred to, Scott appeared right behind my transport caravan. How had he known to be there in that ward, much less that room, just as I was arriving? I saw his face and immediately felt a rush of emotion akin to coming back to your beloved home after a terrible vacation, mixed with the knowledge that everything would be okay now that Scott was there.

I am here and now Scott is here, too.

"Do you know what time it is?" he asked as soon as he was beside me in the room.

I shook my head, no.

"Five-fucking-thirty," he said, pale-faced and with hands shaking as he reached out to touch my cheek.

I was gobsmacked. I cannot begin to comprehend what he went through over those seven and a half hours. I hope with every fibre of my being that our roles are never reversed, with me experiencing the mental torment of waiting so many hours to know that he is okay.

I had yet to really examine the state of my body, either physically or with my own internal processing, but I very deeply wished to be wearing a pair of underwear at that moment. I began attempting to rally the brain power to ask Scott to collect my bag from our car when a nurse came into the room and suggested he do just that. Scott tore his hand and eyes away from me and left as the nurse came farther into the room and introduced herself. All these mundane interactions were happening around me while I was realizing that the wave of nausea I had felt in the recovery room had never subsided. It was less of a wave, it seemed, than a tsunami, and the earthquake that anesthesia created within my body was at that very second crashing forward throughout every part of me.

It's a special experience to meet a new person only to immediately and violently begin vomiting in front of them, but that's exactly how my relationship with this nurse began. Some sign obviously crossed my face before the wave of sickness started because I reared up and folded over as much as the bandages around my chest allowed, and when I opened my eyes, I was on all fours on my hospital bed and there was a pan held below my mouth. I think all nurses may possess this ability to remain calm in the face of such bodily trauma and heinousness, at least all of the ones you'd want to be caring for you immediately after a bilateral mastectomy and whilst vomiting heavily.

After my initial wave of vomiting, I sat back down on the bed knowing that this trauma response had not ended. I told the nurse that I had to get to the bathroom because I desperately needed to pee and also because I knew there was more gastrointestinal carnage coming. The first issue I identified was that I was barefoot, a problem that I immediately disregarded when I noted the speed at which the second wave of the nausea tsunami was advancing forward. The second and significantly more foreign issue was that I'd finally connected the gentle tugging sensation I'd felt to the two drains that were attached to my body.

In the Venn diagram of medically fascinating and medically disgusting, post-surgical drains are at the very centre. On each side of my body, a perforated silicone tube had been fed into the cavity under my skin where each of my breasts had been. The tubes transitioned to clear, unperforated silicone as they snaked their way out of my body, and each tube was sewn into my skin at their exit several centimetres below my mastectomy staples. At their ends, a silicone bulb was collecting the fluid that my body created in response to the massive trauma of the mastectomy. If these drains were to be described without the context of their post-surgical application, anyone would be excused for believing that they were a medieval torture device and not an important surgical advancement.

I sat on the bed, having already forgotten the name of the nurse I had just met and promptly emptied my stomach contents in front of. I was weak from lack of any food all day and I'd needed to pee and vomit with equal desperation, so there existed a very real possibility that any slight hindrance I'd encounter from the drains would be just enough to prevent me from getting to the bathroom in time. I feared there was a strong chance that my weak body would imminently expel fluids from every opening, regardless of my proximity to a toilet.

Perhaps miraculously, but quite likely purposefully, another nurse came into the room and suddenly they were standing on either side of me. Each nurse held a drain while also holding me up, and together they directed me in a shuffle to the bathroom. I immediately vomited again, even more violently than the first time. After I finally, miraculously, felt that there wasn't anything left to expel, I flushed. I wiped my mouth with some single-ply hospital toilet paper, and I sat down to pee, amazed that I managed to retain the contents of my bladder amid all the violent retching.

When I stood up, the nurse next to me had her eyes on the toilet and she uttered a confused, "Ummmmmm . . ."

I turned to follow her gaze and saw that everything that had just been evicted from my bladder was bright green. Perhaps because of my days of peeing orange and red during chemotherapy, this radioactive green colour didn't faze me in the slightest. I shrugged, flushed it all away, and began the shuffle back to my bed.

Seconds after my violent vomiting ended, Scott walked back in the room and I was finally, finally able to put on some underwear. As Scott helped me climb back onto the bed, it occurred to me why my pee was green. The dye that had been injected into my breast that morning had been neon blue, and as it ended its journey through my lymphatic system to be expunged from my body, it had mingled with my average yellow urine before exiting in the usual fashion. Yellow + blue = green. In fact, later that evening, the artificial blue hue became briefly darker and bluer before returning to a standard human yellow tone by the next day. All that was left for me now was to somehow produce violet urine and I'd have pissed an entire rainbow.

Once I was settled in my hospital bed and wearing my undies, Scott and I began comparing notes on our day. As we talked, heat rolled across my body like the oscillation of a fan, yet I didn't pay much attention to the temperature fluctuations. I'd grown weary and accustomed to their company over the previous two months because hot flushes had begun after my third cycle of chemo when I'd stopped ovulating. The worst of the heat blooms would cause me to lose concentration, not be able to carry on a conversation, and shed layers of clothing regardless of the ambient temperature wherever I was. If I was overwhelmed, surprised, or angry, I might have either a particularly intense hot flush or just more throughout the day. The converse was also true, in that a hot flush could leave me with a residual emotional rawness for a few minutes afterwards that felt like I might either cry or snap a pencil in half. As Scott and I sat in my hospital room debriefing on our day, I accepted the logic that the emotional toil of a bilateral mastectomy would be the harbinger of some significant internal fire.

Scott knew he had to head home by six o'clock that evening to help our daughters get to sleep as comfortably as possible with an upended bedtime routine. The heat blooms were continuing to come one after another and I felt physically weak from my hair to my toes. I felt a ringing in my ears, a pounding in my head, and for a few seconds I had to focus on breathing or I felt like my lungs might forget how to expand properly. I told my husband that I was beyond exhausted and that he should go home and I would go to sleep. He got my antianxiety medications together for me, turned on the white-noise app on my phone to block out some of the hospital sounds, and I closed my eyes and tried to pretend I was at home in my own bed. I didn't vomit any more that night, but I rode one hot flush after another all night long.

CHAPTER TWENTY-FOUR

When I woke the next morning, it was very early and I was ravenous. I had packed a bag of food and was dining on candy for breakfast when Scott called to check in and see what I wanted him to bring for breakfast. His parents were staying at our house until my discharge so Scott could spend some portion of each day with me while Ava and Bean would be safe and comfortable in their home.

"Can you bring me one of everything?" I asked, groggily.

"One of everything from where?" he replied.

"Anywhere. Bring me one of everything from any place you decide to go," I responded. Me when I'm hangry is somewhat legendary in our family

"How about a breakfast sandwich, hash brown, coffee?" he suggested.

"Throw in a muffin, too."

"Roger that," he signed off, and I could hear the keys jangling in his hand as he left our house to start the car.

I set my phone back down on the table next to my bed just as a new nurse came into my room. She was bright, refreshed, and carried exactly the energy I needed to feed off of to try and get myself awake and ready to go home.

"Hi Ashleigh!" she began. "How are you feeling this morning?"

"I'm all right, all things considered. I'm not in any pain or anything, but I'm having some intense hot flushes already today," I reported.

"Hot flushes? Okay. Have you been up to visit the bathroom yet this morning?"

"No. Truthfully, some of these heat waves are just flattening me. I don't know if I feel confident to walk to the bathroom and back without help."

"Say no more. Let's get you up to empty your bladder and the post-surgical drains, okay?" She smiled as she said this and came to stand beside me as I swung my feet off the side of the bed. She helped me safely and effectively empty all the overfull vessels in and on my body while ensuring I maintained as much dignity as could be hoped for. Once she helped me get settled back in my bed, she began to record my vitals and explained that I should expect to see a doctor during the morning rounds. That person would make the decision on whether I could be discharged from the hospital that day.

As the nurse was putting away the thermometer and reaching for my arm, I felt yet another heat bloom begin. It crested at the top of my head and crashed downward over my body as she was affixing a blood pressure cuff. I briefly wondered if the presence of a hot flush would alter the data she was recording, but I could not vocalize that thought and remained silent as I watched the cuff inflate. We waited, and then the nurse looked at the monitor quizzically.

"I'm going to take that a second time. Just to confirm the numbers," she told me, using the tone of forced calm I had heard so often from medical professionals discovering an anomaly within me.

It was at that moment that it finally, finally dawned on me that the hot flushes I was experiencing were not really like the ones I had become accustomed to during the months of chemotherapy and recovery. At the same moment that she understood something was wrong, it occurred to me that I should have said something to the nursing staff the evening before about the rolling heat I was experiencing.

"Your blood pressure is low. Very low," she updated me. Her voice was calm but also precise, and her attention was firmly focused on the monitor attached to the cuff.

"I'm going to page your surgeon. There is nothing to be immediately alarmed about. I'll be back in just a few minutes," she told me in staccato phrases.

Seconds after the first nurse exited the room, another nurse came in and stood at my bedside to keep me company, but also to monitor my vitals as we waited for the surgeon to arrive. Minutes passed slowly, but in a remarkably short time the surgeon that had performed my mastectomy the day before was in my room and standing at the foot of my bed.

"You again," I said.

"Same to you," he responded.

"What's going on?" I asked, fear immediately replacing the sarcasm of my greeting.

"Based on your blood pressure and descriptions of how you're feeling, I believe you have a bleed in the surgery site. Your blood pressure is dropping repeatedly because the cavity is filling with blood that cannot be recirculated back throughout your heart and lungs."

"Fuck," I said.

With medical jargon being exchanged from one health care professional to another, a nurse began to unwrap the bandages around my chest. She worked carefully but quickly and in such a way that I could not see my chest after it had been fully uncovered. As soon as the final layer of bandages began to lift, the nurse removing them said something to the effect of: "Oh, okay. Yes." My surgeon calmly indicated to my right side and said that the bleed was clearly on that side because it looked as if I still had a breast mound.

"You have a bleed. Some part of the work done on your right side has not clotted properly and it has continued to bleed. That unchecked bleeding has caused a hematoma on the right side of your chest." He remained calm, controlled, and patient while explaining this to me. "These things happen. It can be fixed either with a wait-and-see approach or with a second surgery to reopen the area, evacuate the pooled blood, find the problem, and fix it with fresh stitches."

"Is this slightly unfortunate or very terrible? How worried should I be?" I asked.

"It's not ideal, but it's also not life threatening when you're in a hospital already."

"Right. Okay," I stammered, thinking about the options set before me. "I'd prefer to absolutely know that it has been fixed," I finally declared with as much confidence as I could gather while actively processing the need for a second surgery so soon.

"I agree. I would have encouraged you to consider that route if you were unsure," he shared. "You are in need of swift addressing; however, you are safely in a hospital room under the close monitoring of nurses and there are multiple surgeons in the building. This is vital, but at the moment it is not an emergency situation."

"I guess there's no chance it'll happen really soon and I can go home today?" I asked, suspecting the answer before I'd even asked the question.

"You're not going home today. The hematoma surgery will happen today and by tomorrow we will know whether it has been successful in stopping the bleeding. We'll have a discussion tomorrow to determine whether you can be discharged."

While I talked with the surgeon, Scott had been texting updates on how close he was with my breakfast. He texted again as the conversation with my surgeon was concluding to say that he was parking and that I would have breakfast and hot coffee in front of me soon.

"Since we don't know when an operating room will be available today, we should assume that you could get the call any hour," the surgeon carried on. "You'll begin fasting immediately in preparation for the hematoma surgery, so that your stomach will be as empty as possible as soon as there's an operating room and a surgery team available for your procedure."

The McBreakfast that was being walked across the parking lot at that very minute was not going to be consumed by me after all.

"Fuuuuuuuck no!" I replied, and then immediately began negotiating a treaty in which I would agree not to eat anything after mid-morning in preparation for my surgery if I could inhale the meal that I could practically smell, it was already so close to the room.

Deal.

My oncology surgeon met Scott in the hallway outside the elevators on the ward, Scott with my breakfast in hand. The surgeon knew who Scott was and filled him in fully on what was happening and what course of action I had opted for. As a foundational member of my cancer care team, there was a rapport between my husband and many of the oncologists and chemotherapy nurses who had been delivering my care since the very beginning. Having medical professionals who were saving my life and who also knew who my partner was on sight meant so much to me. As the patient who was trusting these people to make the best decisions possible regarding my disease, it was heartening to see that they cared about me enough to remember who my personal support system was as well.

Scott came into the room and practically threw the food at me. After the discussion in the hallway, he was already up to speed on my pre-surgery fasting negotiation and he understood the urgency for me to eat breakfast immediately. Over the course of the next twenty minutes, I ate my breakfast, as well as an oatcake and some chocolate-covered almonds at a superhuman speed, all while wrapped in gauze from clavicle to belly button and with two post-surgical drains coiled in my lap collecting my bodily fluids. I was still bald from the chemotherapy treatments I had finished just twenty-four days before, and I had not showered since the very early hours of the previous morning. It was an exceedingly elegant meal.

CHAPTER TWENTY-FIVE

After I had inhaled my breakfast practically without chewing it, another nurse came into the room and helped me empty the drains on both sides of my body for the first time by myself. I had not done this on my own the entire evening before owing to the fact that I was busy bleeding internally, but since that problem would be addressed sometime later that day it was high time for me to take on the management of the torture devices that I would be carrying along in my custom-made T-shirt sidecar pockets for the next few weeks. Post-surgical drains are undoubtedly a medical marvel for their ability to reduce the likelihood of an abscess or an infection, but they are also indisputably a medieval torture device because the person with them has to carry around a container filling with their own bodily fluids for weeks.

"Have you ever owned a fish tank?" the nurse asked me before we began the lesson on emptying post-surgical drains.

"Yeah, actually, I have!" I replied, confused but, by this point, also nonplussed by any analogy used during explanations of cancer treatment and recovery.

"Well, the mechanism of how these drains remove fluid from inside your surgery site is very similar to how a fish tank siphon works to clean the bottom of a tank," she said, chuckling. All of my favourite medical professionals can openly laugh at the absolute absurdity of some of the methods humans have come up with to improve outcomes in medicine.

"One end of the drain line is coiled inside the surgery site and the silicone tubing is sewn into your skin at the place where it exits your torso," she explained.

"The stitching at the exit spot is uncomfortable," I said. The drains were almost undetectable when they were resting in the pockets of my shirt or pants, but if the lines got pulled upwards or hung without support, the stitches holding them into my body stretched painfully.

"Most people report that the exit site is the most uncomfortable place. Not only because of the stitches, but also because your body recognizes the foreign object and the skin gets irritated around the tubes as the body tries to get rid of them," she explained. "The end of the drain outside your body has that bulb attached to it that collects the fluid removed from your chest and, just like the fish tank siphon, we need to apply suction to the end we want the fluid to collect at so that it can be sucked up and out of the space where we don't want it," she explained.

As she was giving me this fish tank analogy, she was also moving the blankets at my side to find the end of the tubing that had disappeared under the bedding around me. There was one drain on each side of my body, and she selected the silicone bulb that was holding the fluid exiting the right side. This is the side of my body that was bleeding without clotting and that would be operated on for a second time later that day, and the bulb was more than half filled with deep red blood. The sight was startling to behold.

"Holy crow!" I exclaimed. "That's a lot of blood!"

"It is. This bulb needs to be emptied now. When the bulb on

the end is this full, the siphon is less effective at pulling the blood and fluid out of your surgical site. That's when you need to empty the bulb and increase the suction on the lines," she explained.

I was reeling at this latest oddity of surgical recovery.

"You pop the small opening here." She opened a small, sealed spout at the top of the drain as she said this, "and then pour the contents into a small measuring cup like this one." She picked up a small disposable cup from the rolling side table positioned near the bed. It was one of those small, translucent-white disposable cups that medications are delivered to patients in. It had graded markings around the outside that could be used to note the gram and cubic centimetre amounts of liquid inside.

"After you've emptied the contents, squeeze the bulb together to make it as flat as possible by pushing out all the air," she explained as she squeezed the bulb in her hand and replaced the cap on the spout. "Now the suction of the compressed bulb will work to pull the liquid out of your chest cavity. It's working better already, see?" She indicated to the drain line as it snaked across the sheets towards the bulb in her hand. The contents in the line had become markedly darker already, and we watched as a couple of small drops fell to the bottom of the bulb.

"That pace will slow once the excess fluid is pulled up and out. It will also slow considerably more after the surgery to correct the bleed happens," she told me. "Now, the final step for this side is to record the fluid output and dispose of it," she casually concluded.

"I have to record it," I stated, snorting at the hilarity of collecting data with a medieval torture device.

"Yes," she confirmed, smiling.

"She's 100 per cent going to make a spreadsheet to record the data," Scott tattled to her.

"If you can think of a better method to keep track of data, I'd like to hear it!" I retorted.

"I love that you haven't even heard why you record the amounts, you're just fully committed to doing it," Scott said back with a laugh.

"I'm sure there's a solid science-based reason!" I said to him. "Please tell me there's a good reason," I said quietly, turning to the nurse.

"Of course," she reported with enthusiasm. "Every person's body creates fluid of varying volumes over varying amounts of time, so there isn't a universal amount of time the drains should be in. Instead, the drains can be removed when fluid production has become reduced enough that your circulatory and lymphatic systems can fully take on the task of removing the fluid without the drains lightening the volume load. Thirty cc's of fluid is where that threshold is low enough for your body to take over; so you're recording to see when you get to that point," she informed us.

"See, that's why," I said and kissed the air in Scott's direction.

"I did not doubt your spreadsheet dedication for a moment," he responded, sending a kiss back.

All three of us were laughing by that point.

"Let's see what the output is like from the drain on the other side and this time, you do the emptying," she suggested. "Once you note the amount, you can dispose of the fluid by flushing it," she concluded, answering my next question before I'd even asked it.

I emptied the second drain and found that dramatically less fluid was being expelled from the side of my body that had been clotting properly after the mastectomy. While I was emptying the bulb and recording the fluid like a pro, the nurse and I discussed the signs of infection I should be keeping an eye out for in the days ahead. She also showed me how to squeeze the lines to move fluid down to the bulbs and advised me that as I healed, it would be normal to see small blood clots in the drain lines. This conversation was not as surreal as the ones I had had with the nurses administering The Red Devil into my heart while in full medical armour, but it was damn close.

With my stomach full and my drains empty, Scott and I finally had an unhurried stretch of time to reconnect about the previous day, the developments that morning, and also how our kiddos were faring without me. While we were catching up, Scott pointed out that we had both noticed the output from the drain on my right side—the side with the bleed—was dramatically higher than the output from the left side before he'd gone home the previous evening. In what would be a conversation repeated multiple times over the course of the next year, Scott berated himself for not realizing that something was going wrong inside me that could not be explained away as hot flushes. Somehow, in his rush to see me lucid and alive and then get home in time to comfort our kids while they fell asleep, he expected himself to be able to accurately diagnose a complication of a major medical procedure—a major medical procedure that neither of us had ever come close to truly knowing anything about before that very day. I understood how he felt, because I would have felt the same way if I was in his position, but I could also see how ludicrous that expectation was and pointed it out immediately. The people who were supposed to realize something dangerous was going on—the nurses and my surgeon—knew practically as soon as the blood pressure cuff inflated, and they immediately sprang to action. I was clearly in a safe place and, while I was not quite yet on the road to recovery, I soon would be.

It was during this conversation that it occurred to me that the hot flushes, ear ringing, and head pounding that I had been experiencing did not start until after I had been vomiting the day before. It would have taken some time for a single busted stitch or vessel that did not clot properly to allow enough blood to escape my circulatory system before I began feeling the effects of blood loss. The exact cause of my internal bleeding was not relevant to my ultimate prognosis; however, the violent sickness I had experienced just hours after my surgery undeniably may have impacted the bleeding that came later, either as its cause or merely as a factor that exacerbated it.

Scott hadn't been in the room when I was sick, so he didn't have the experience of seeing just how hard I'd been purging, but when I told him it was worse than the few times I vomited while recovering from chemotherapy treatment, it gave him an image of the high bar I'd surpassed. The possibility that my profuse vomiting was the cause of the bleed has resulted in me being especially diligent in discussing sedation options that might mitigate nausea with all the anesthesiologists I would meet with after my mastectomy. My philosophy became one of doing everything medically possible to slow the anaesthetic earthquake before it became a heaving tsunami.

I may be painting a picture of an alert and upright human who could conversationally spar with her husband and feast on takeout, but the reality was that the periods of bottoming-out blood pressure continued unabated, and I required help just to get to my feet. I slept most of the morning, I needed help to move to an upright sitting position, and I practically had to be carried to the bathroom. I was clearly in need of intervention before the surgery could be carried out and that intervention was a blood transfusion.

The nurse that administered the transfusion stayed with me in my hospital room for the first twenty minutes of my body accepting the donated blood in order to watch for signs of rejection. I was hooked up to the IV via my port for the transfusion, making the whole process painless without even an IV line tugging at my hand while it was happening. I felt no better and no worse physically as I received this gift of blood. Emotionally, I felt immense gratitude that the process of infusing my depleted body with blood was so easy to accomplish here in my hospital bed that it almost felt routine. Some person at some time had decided to sit in a chair at a Canadian Blood Services branch and allow their blood to be collected and banked, and because that selfless event happened I was now able to lay in my hospital bed and receive that blood as I waited for a surgeon and an operating room to be available at the same time. Without that blood being available to replenish me, my situation could have been significantly more dire.

Scott and I waited throughout that afternoon and received updates as they were conveyed to the nursing staff throughout the day. As the afternoon gave way to evening, I was very grateful that the terms of my surgical treaty from that morning had allowed me to eat breakfast. As it neared time for Scott to leave and go home for our daughters' bedtime, I had received one transfusion, slept off and on all day, but did not yet have a definitive time for my hematoma surgery to take place. So, of course, immediately after Scott and I agreed that he needed to leave to be with Ava and Bean, a nurse came by to say that an operating room was being prepped for me.

My surgery was expected to take only twenty minutes once I was sedated; however, the process of getting to that point would take time, and then I'd have to wake up and be transported back to my room again. I needed Scott to be there when I was wheeled out of the hospital room and also to be there when I was wheeled back in so I could focus on the moment that I got to see him again and feel that flood of safety and comfort. But our kids also needed him at home in our bed beside them, reading books and giving them that same feeling of safety and comfort. There was no discussion needed, he left right then and went home to be with them.

Minutes after Scott left, I was helped into a wheelchair to be transported to the operating room a few floors below my hospital bed. That time, I was the only patient sitting in the chairs outside the operating room doors, so I had no other person with whom to exchange the strained smile of anticipation mixed with resignation that so often passes between patients with cancer in waiting rooms. It was now after seven o'clock in the evening and all of the people present were taking part in my hematoma evacuation surgery. Being the only patient sitting in the waiting area made me consider what the space would feel like when there was absolutely no one there.

Did the ceiling vent make that rhythmic squeaking noise all night long?

Did the last person out of the unit turn off the lights, or was it neon and bright in there all day and all night too?

Would the antiseptic smell seem sharper if there weren't people in hospital gowns and scrubs there to visually explain why sterility was necessary?

My wait was a short one. Once again, I found myself closing my eyes in one second only to wake the very next second, an hour later. Again, I was the only patient in the recovery space accompanied by two nurses watching me attentively as I struggled to open my eyes. They told me everything had gone well, it was all finished and I was rebandaged.

There are no memories within me of the transport back to my hospital room after that surgery, and if the anesthesia caused me to feel nauseous, I was not aware enough to realize it. My final memory of that evening was of a nurse coming into my room with the bags of blood I was to receive during my second blood transfusion of the day. I asked her if it was okay for me to sleep through the transfusion, she said yes, and I powered down immediately.

CHAPTER TWENTY-SIX

When I awoke the next morning, sunlight was streaming into my hospital room. My very first thought as I came to consciousness was *holy crap*. Not because I felt awful and not because I needed to pee and couldn't get to the bathroom, nor because I was having yet another hot flush—I swore inside my head when I compared the bottomless chasm of physiological difference between the way I had felt when I had closed my eyes the previous night and the way I felt then as I opened my eyes eight hours later. Whether it was the deep sleep, the blood transfusion, or the finally addressed internal bleed, I felt so much better that I was retroactively scared by how awful I had felt the day before. Just as the severity of my carcinoma had been made more obvious when chemotherapy began to reduce it, the severity of how awful I had felt the previous day was easier to see when looking backwards.

Minutes before the needle on my second blood transfusion pierced the skin above my port the previous evening, I'd called Scott and told him that I was out of surgery, back in my hospital room, and was already approximately one-third asleep. I awoke for the second day after my bilateral mastectomy once again with a call from my husband asking what I wanted him to bring me for breakfast.

When he walked through the doorway to my hospital room on that day, it was not to be greeted by a wife flattened in her hospital bed and unable to do so much as sit up independently; rather, I was standing at the foot of the hospital bed looking out the fifth-floor window, having just watched him cross the parking lot and head into the front entrance of the hospital. I gleefully reached out for my breakfast as he stared at me with an expression of shock and relief that confirmed my own assessment of how much better I was faring.

"Hi!" I said in greeting, both to my husband and also to the piping hot coffee he handed me.

Scott replied with: "Holy shit."

Before I'd had my mastectomy, I had been under anesthesia twice in my lifetime: once to have a scope put down my esophagus when I was thirteen—an experience I have no memory of—and once when I had my wisdom teeth removed at nineteen. Both experiences were so far in my past and so minor in their recovery processes and overall impact on my life, both beforehand and afterwards, that they offered absolutely no education on what I should have expected in the hours and days after a surgery as significant in scope and effect as a bilateral mastectomy. Of course, I had attributed some of my body's reactions the previous day to the fact that I had a complication inside the cavity of my surgery site, but I also assumed some of the lethargy, discomfort, sweating, head pounding, and lack of focus was because of the mastectomy itself. It turns out that once the bleed inside my chest was addressed and the blood that it had spilled was replaced, every debilitating bodily effect that I had felt had been caused by the hematoma. I felt perfectly fine! I was still bandaged from my collarbone to my belly button and I still had two drains protruding from my body, but when I was sitting down in a comfortable position that supported both my back and my drains, I felt almost normal.

My IV tree was outfitted with a locked box around a narcotic pump that enabled me to self-administer medication whenever I needed it to help manage my pain. The pump had a dosage recorder on it that the hospital staff could access to see how much of the pain medication I'd needed, and when. At the time of my discharge from the hospital, I hadn't needed any narcotic pain management medications at all. I do not say this to present myself as a medical martyr—rest assured, if I had needed those medications, I would have utilized that narcotic pump to the fullest—I just didn't need significant pain management after this particular surgery. Perhaps the minor discomforts I felt here and there that I mitigated with some acetaminophen would have seemed more intense if I had not just come through thirty-six hours of slow internal bleeding, who knows. But for whatever reason, I was awake, alert, and ready to go home as soon as Scott walked through my hospital room door that morning.

It was another day full of waiting, but I was finally discharged from the hospital around six o'clock that evening. Immediately prior to being discharged, several doctors and surgeons came into my room to review my recovery and go over my limitations for the following few weeks. As it happened, one of the doctors was the surgical resident who had stood beside me as I cried before being sedated for my first surgery.

She remembered me immediately. Without prompting, she told me that my breast had received the salute and send-off it rightly deserved, just as I had asked. I rode the joy from that knowledge all the way home. In fact, I still have that joy within me to this day.

CHAPTER TWENTY-SEVEN

Over the course of the following two weeks, a community health nurse came to my home every few days to change the bandages across my chest and monitor the fluid volume from the drains. Ten days post-surgery, I was able to have one drain removed. The process of removing a post-surgical drain is significantly worse in the imagination than it is in reality, as it took literally seconds for me to be freed of the nuisance. The nurse snipped the stitches that were wrapped around the silicone line and threaded through my skin, counted to three, and pulled it out. I was absolutely shocked at how much of the drain was inside my body—there was at least thirty centimetres of tubing! The relief at having even one of those devices removed from my body was intoxicating.

Initially after my mastectomy, I had had multiple layers of gauze and bandages wrapped across the incisions and drain exit sites, but over the days of bandage changes by the community health nurse, the amount of necessary dressings was reduced significantly. By the time the second medieval torture device was removed, I was down to several long bandages across my chest, primarily applied to prevent the staples from getting hooked on my clothing. It's not possible to shower with post-surgical drains in, so I had been exclusively taking baths since returning home; however, even then, I was not able to fully grasp the change my body had undergone, as the barrier of bandages hid the absence of what once was and I looked away whenever those barriers were removed by the nurse.

Sixteen days after my bilateral mastectomy, a nurse came into my home to remove the final drain, all the staples, and the remaining bandages on my body; I was hesitant about what discomfort I would feel as the staples were removed, and I was even more trepidatious about the discomfort I would feel without a bandage wall between my flat chest and my knowing brain. There would be no more excuse to not know exactly how different my body looked and felt. It was fucking go time.

The nurse removed the drain first and I was finally able to lay down comfortably without fear of squashing a drain bulb with disgusting consequences. Despite the fact that I had purposefully looked away at every bandage change prior to that day, that final time I intended to look at my own chest as the staples were removed. As bandages were peeled back, my first shock was seeing the craters where my breasts used to live. I had assumed that the bandage had been adding just a thin layer of excess to my skin; however, once the padding of those armpit-to-armpit bandages was removed, it was revealed that the bandages themselves had been compensating for a significant amount of the deficiency across my chest.

Underneath the bandages, I had a red, bumpy, pinched scar line starting at one armpit and running horizontally across my chest. It stopped midway across, leaving a gap of several centimetres with no trauma, before the scar that is the headstone marking the death of my second breast started. This scar continued across to the opposite armpit. My second shock was the sheer number of staples that had been holding my skin together under the cover of the bandages. The incision scars were pulled together and held by staples all across the battlefield of my chest, some perfectly even across the scar and others slightly grown in and with dried blood at their roots. The sight of my own chest for the first time in sixteen days was shocking for the violence it displayed. This visual evidence of brutality stood testament to what was necessary for me to overcome cancer.

A surgical staple looks just like a staple you'd find in an office supply store, though slightly thicker and ideally significantly more sterile. A surgical staple remover also looks similar to a staple remover that you'd find in an office supply store and, again, hopefully significantly more sterile. Each staple was removed individually, and the process was mostly painless because nerve damage across my chest meant I could feel virtually nothing within several centimetres or so above and below my incision scar. This five-centimetre expanse of my chest remains desensitized to this day.

To be stapled together as a human feels as sharp and utilitarian as the word staple is. Each move and twist of the upper body pulls one side of the staple against the other in a tug-of-war played out through the skin that does not lend itself to comfortable movement in any direction. As soon as my skin was no longer impaled by metal staples or silicone tubing, my mobility increased dramatically. I counted as the nurse worked from left to right across my body, and she had removed a total of seventy-seven staples by the time she was finished.

I shed more than one tear over the landscape of my body after my mastectomy, but I never again looked at my chest with the hatred that I had carried around while my breast was present after my diagnosis. It continues to be a complicated relationship to have with my own breasts but remains one that does not include any regret for my decision to have a bilateral mastectomy.

CHAPTER TWENTY-EIGHT

After my cancerous right breast was removed, it was sent to the pathology department of the Cancer Centre to be fully dismantled and examined. Three lymph nodes were also sent through the same process, as well as my presumably non-cancerous left breast. The pathology report can be both the bane and the blessing of the life of any patient because it is an explanation of the scientific measuring of the causes and effects of a disease. In the case of cancer, it can tell a patient that they are going to survive or that there is nothing more that can be done. This is not to suggest that it's an either/or relationship, of course, as there are an abundance of stops along this pathological pathway.

I ran the arduous marathon of diagnostic imaging and then chemotherapy only to pass that finish line and end up on an operating table, and my first post-surgical pathology report promised to be half a dozen pages of scientific evidence that validated or refuted the steps I'd taken during that marathon.

I expected I would hear the details of the pathology report at my six-week post-operative check-up with my oncology surgeon in early January. It was, therefore, a total shock to arrive for an appointment with my medical oncologist on December 23rd and see that she had the full report literally in hand and ready to share.

"I know you want all the details in here," she told Scott and me as she indicated the pathology printouts in her hand. "But do you want the conclusion first?"

"Yes," Scott and I said in unison, breathless and terrified in equal measure.

"I am not emotionally prepared for whatever you're about to say," I added. As always, I was sitting on the exam table with my shoes and shirt off and a hospital gown covering the bright red scar across my chest. The sight of the pathology pages in her hand caused my ears to ring and my vision to blur.

"If it's good news, I want it immediately so we can celebrate," Scott told me.

"If it's bad news?" I asked, looking at the floor. Was I about to cause the emotional destruction of my husband again?

"It isn't bad," the oncologist broke in with a smile on her face, pre-empting Scott's answer before we could consider what we would do if we left that room with the knowledge that more carcinomas had been found in my right breast or infiltrating my chest wall. "Overall, it's very good."

"Oh thank fuck," Scott said, gently pulling me into him as he stood beside the examination table. I rested my forehead on his chest, spent and exhilarated at the unexpected emotional roller coaster of this news. Pathology isn't only the measurement of the causes and effects of disease, it is also the measurement of how much fight a cancer patient has gone through—details include scars, calcifications, inflammation—and receiving a pathology report depletes the patient just from waiting to hear what has been discovered. This pathology report was a measurement of the fight behind me, and it was also an indicator of what would still be ahead. What was going on in my lymph nodes? Were the tumour margins large? What additional treatments needed to be considered? I was without drains, staples, or bandages at that appointment, yet I felt exposed and unprepared as I listened to a slice-by-slice assessment of the cancer that had dominated my life for over a year.

"Your pathology report details how the invasive ductal carcinomas in your right breast shrunk to an almost immeasurably small size following chemotherapy. What was once classified as a grade 3 collection of cancerous carcinomas was reduced to just two tumours, one measuring at two millimetres and one at three millimetres," my medical oncologist paraphrased from the report. "There were also scattered small spots remaining of the DCIS behind the right nipple."

"Okay," I said, still absorbing.

"You did not have a complete pathological response—basically chemotherapy was not fully effective at eliminating the cancer from the breast because these small tumours were still measurable under a microscope," she continued. "However, a complete response is not necessary for a pathology report to be glowing as far as effectiveness of pre-surgery treatment goes. I am very happy to see significantly reduced carcinomas with large margins of healthy tissue in this pathology report."

"Okay!" I said, more confidently this time.

"We can see that chemotherapy worked at stopping growth and also dramatically reducing the size of the carcinomas in your breast, which makes it likely that it had the same effect on any small collections of cancer cells that migrated outside of your breast through your lymph nodes. I can't stress enough that this report is excellent in that regard," her tone changed slightly now and she was clearly choosing her words carefully.

"Is this a 'but' I feel coming on?" Scott's posture stiffened beside me.

"No, not a 'but'. More like . . . a pause. A pathology report is most often a mixed bag, and this one is no exception. All of the lymph nodes removed were found to contain deposits of breast cancer cells. The collection of cells found were sizable, and their presence needs to be discussed."

"How sizable?" I asked.

"Each node contained a deposit of breast cancer cells that were between three and four and a half millimetres in size," she replied, consulting the report for the exact measurements.

"Wait, the deposits in my breast were only two and three millimetres," I immediately responded. "That means . . ." I paused to decipher what was being indicated by these numbers. "There was more cancer found in my lymph nodes than in the entirety of my right breast."

"Keep in mind that all of the cancer cells found in the nodes were the same type found in the breast. We know that based on the examination of those cells," the oncologist was quick to clarify. "Although a more measurable tumour was found in the nodes, it is still the same exact kind of cancer. Additionally, your left breast was entirely cancer free."

"But with its own series of battle wounds amassed during the rounds of chemotherapy, I'm sure. My digestive system barely made it through the TAC intact."

"You were never going to keep the left breast anyway. Guilt by association with the right one, I think you said," Scott reminded me.

"This is not insurmountable, Ashleigh. The most important fact we wanted to see is here—evidence that chemotherapy caused a dramatic reduction in carcinoma size. That gold star is weighted much more than the finding of residual cells in your lymph nodes is able to diminish," the doctor reminded us.

"What's next?" I asked.

How many times have I come through a terrible ordeal only to ask "what's next?"

"You'll go back and see your surgeon for consultation on next steps based on the lymph node findings, but as far as medical oncology is concerned, you do not need to consider chemotherapy treatments again," she informed us.

It can be difficult to decide whether a pathology report is cause for celebration or consolation, and most often it's a combination of both. Even with the sections of my pathology report detailing the findings in my lymph nodes, this report was sublime. The news of chemotherapy efficacy allowed me to release the fear of having to begin a new chemotherapy regime. Enduring five and a half months of chemotherapy treatments and recovery was the worst experience of my life; any medical report that informed me I did not need to go through that experience again was a shining positive in my mind.

CHAPTER TWENTY-NINE

My post-surgical check-up occurred in the first week of January, and it was there that my oncology surgeon told me I needed to consider another surgery. Six weeks earlier, we had discussed the pros and cons of having a sentinel node biopsy instead of taking an all-or-nothing approach to the removal of my lymph nodes during my mastectomy. The sentinel node branch of the surgical decision tree offered the possibility of maintaining the functionality of my lymphatic system while also being able to take a peek at the progression of the cancer that had already been found in that area. I'd known that I was rolling the dice on the chance that all of the nodes removed could contain cancer cells, and it was clear that I had not come out on top with that bet. I needed to decide what to do with that reality now.

I could opt to forgo surgery and keep the remaining lymph nodes, and I'd still possibly never endure a cancer diagnosis again. It was likely that the chemotherapy had eviscerated any cancer cells that made it out of the lymphatic chain leading from my breast, and it was possible that the nodes that had already been removed housed all of the cancerous cells that remained in my axillary nodes after chemotherapy. In addition to the general risks of any surgery, the removal of my remaining lymph nodes carried with it a selection of possible complications unique to that procedure, and all of those risks combined could ultimately be undertaken for no demonstrable benefit.

The surgeon presented me with all the relevant information on what the presence of cancer in the sentinel nodes that had been removed meant, gave me his unrestrained opinion on what he felt should be done, and left the decision on how to proceed up to me. I did not hesitate. I did not call Scott to confer. I did not need to contemplate any aspect of the position I was in. Those remaining lymph nodes were coming out lest the next one or any other along the chain of that superhighway contained even a single cell with intentions on dividing too fast. I would not lie awake at night and wonder.

"Fuck, I'm having more surgery aren't I?"

One beat after I spoke, my surgeon pointed at the calendar on the wall behind him and said, "I have you booked for a right axillary lymph node dissection on the morning of Friday, January 17th."

He'd led me to the water but knew I had to take that drink myself.

CHAPTER THIRTY

January 17th was just over a week after the discussion with my oncology surgeon, and during that week I once again grieved the imminent loss of a part of my body, though this time I was grieving more for an impending loss of functionality than for a visual change. I stocked the fridge and freezer and packed the hospital bag, this time packing for a two-night stay in the hospital, even though my surgeon was hopeful that I would be recovered sufficiently to be discharged the same day as the procedure. My mastectomy experience taught me to pack for the worst-case scenario, and then pack a little more. Plus add one more pair of underwear. Once again, my in-laws came to stay the day beforehand, and my kids were prepared for the possibility of being without me for a night.

I arrived at the hospital for my pre-admission appointment on Thursday, the day before my surgery was scheduled to be carried out. Again, I met with a nurse to discuss expectations around recovery and restrictions on physical abilities, I had blood drawn, I met with a physiotherapist to review exercises to begin after surgery. Through another dose of karmic kismet, when I sat to wait for my number to be called in the blood collection department, there was a fellow breast cancer survivor sitting in the chair next to me. She was also going through pre-admission for a surgery she was having the following week. She noticed my port and struck up a conversation about her own experience with breast cancer by sharing that she was finally listening to her internal voice and getting prosthetic breast implants some five years after her own mastectomy. Connecting with another breast cancer fighter, and hearing that one day I would stop lying awake at night staring at the ceiling wondering if cancer was coursing through my body, was exactly what I needed that day. I had been feeling particularly beaten down by cancer before this surgery.

The complete loss of lymph nodes in my axillary area meant that my right arm would be losing nearly all of its connection to my lymphatic system. The lymphatic system operates one of those bodily processes that we tend not to appreciate until it's malfunctioning. It's a circulatory network of nodes and vessels that runs all around the body from the head to the toes, with the responsibility of overseeing lymph fluid levels and distribution throughout the body. The lymphatic system collects the fluid that has drained from the blood into the surrounding tissues and returns it back into the blood to be reused, or passes it on to the waste systems for it to be expelled from the body. Lymph fluid helps fight infection and speed up the scabbing process at the site of a skin break, so the lymphatic system plays a key role in moderating infection risk. There are collections of nodes at the clavicle and around the ribcage, so my torso and neck would continue to avail of the full abilities of my lymphatic network, but once the axillary dissection was complete, my right arm would lose its most effective player in lymphatic distribution.

After surgery, lymph fluid would continue to be produced as this process occurs in the bone marrow; however, the ability for my right arm to dispose of the lymph fluid when too much had accumulated would be severely hampered. If I were to cut my right arm or develop any kind of infection, my body would spring into action and flood the site with blood and lymph fluid in order to help mitigate infection and begin the healing process, without knowing that the excess fluid had very minimal routes to depart the site afterwards. When this fluid collects and cannot find a pathway back to regular circulation throughout my body, swelling occurs and it can be difficult to reverse. If the fluid build-up cannot drain before a skin break heals, this lack of drainage can ironically have an intensifying effect: instead of flushing the site of bacteria, the trapped lymph fluid can form a kind of cesspool under the skin around an injury, which makes abscesses and cellulitis a risk. It is a situation where an ounce of prevention is worth more than a pound of cure, and preventing swelling and infection in my right arm is something I will be conscious of for the remainder of my life.

All these irreversible internal changes were on my mind as I spoke with the breast cancer fighter seated next to me in the blood collection department. She understood my path because she had been down it before. Hearing from someone a few years ahead of me on that path who was alive, navigating survivorship post-cancer, and still moving forward was just the antidote I needed for my current poisoned mindset.

Once I finished my blood work, I returned to the pre-admission department to meet with the nurse once again, followed by the anesthesiologist to discuss the plan for my sedation with the goal of preventing post-surgical nausea by every means possible. We also discussed what to do if the weather showed up as harshly as was called for the next day. On the day before my scheduled surgery, the forecast predicted that eastern Newfoundland might see forty to sixty centimetres of snowfall in a single day. I live in a climate that is no stranger to significant snowfall, ice, rain, and wind, sometimes all at once. For six months of the year, ice and snow are a significant factor in travelling, and road conditions are in the back of the minds of anyone driving during the peak winter months. We carry on through the weather because we're accustomed to snow; however, forty to sixty centimetres of snowfall in one day was dramatic even for communities full of people with hands well calloused by the handles of snow shovels.

I'd talked to my surgeon's office the previous day when the forecast initially suggested thirty to forty-five centimetres might fall, and I was told that a non-elective surgery had never been cancelled due to forecasted weather. Since my surgery was non-elective, it would be going ahead as scheduled unless I myself could not be present.

At pre-admission, I repeated what I had been told on the phone by the surgeon's reception staff but asked again for clarity on storm cancellations since the forecasted accumulation had already increased significantly in just twenty-four hours. It seemed clear that a blizzard was headed for us and I didn't want to show up at the hospital in the morning only to find out my procedure had been rescheduled. I told the nurse that I would be there the next morning; however, because I was scheduled to arrive at seven o'clock and the hospital doors opened at the same time, how would I know if the surgery was cancelled? I heard the same refrain: non-elective surgery is not going to be cancelled because of inclement weather. I could take the hint.

I went home to make sure the flashlights had batteries and the generator was filled with gas in case the power went out, and then packed my hospital bag—extra underwear and all—into my Subaru. Scott would assuredly get me to the hospital the next day even if the forecast of more than forty centimetres of snow did materialize. With an arrival time of 7 a.m. and a surgery time of 8:30 a.m., coupled with a relatively short procedure, I wondered if maybe Scott and I could even be heading home before the worst of the wind and snow began. That way, we could ride out what would probably be the worst snowstorm of our winter season back at home with our kids and my in-laws.

CHAPTER THIRTY-ONE

I woke the next morning to howling winds with some snow falling, but nothing that would cause me to pause and wonder if I shouldn't be heading out that morning. Bean woke up when my alarm went off and we had some extra snuggles in bed together on the off chance that I would need to be admitted after surgery. Scott and I departed early in case we encountered delays en route, and we could see the snow falling heavier and feel the wind blowing harder over the course of the twenty minutes it took to drive to the hospital. We parked around 6:45 a.m. and prepared to walk towards the same building along the same path we had taken so many times before. The parking lot was practically empty—a benefit of being extremely early on the surgery schedule—and we were able to park in the row of spaces closest to the front of the hospital.

"You should probably just bring the bag in now," I said to Scott as I shut my door.

"Yeah, I thought so too. I'll probably wait in the surgery waiting room this time. It'll be so much less time away from you for this one," he replied as he opened the back door of our vehicle to grab my bag. The wind pushed against the door with such ferocity he had to wedge his body in the gap to keep the door open as he gathered the overnight bag. "Comparatively less time, I mean. It's still going to suck," he yelled over the wind.

"I'm also going to want to put on clean clothing as soon as my arms can manage co-ordinating it," I reminded him.

He still had the upper half of his body inside the car when I heard him calling out over the sound of the howling wind, "What about the snacks? And the blanket?"

"Leave them," I called back, "I'll only need that stuff if I have to stay the night."

"True," he said, extracting himself from the vehicle and watching as the door was slammed shut by the wind. Scott took my hand and we sprinted across the empty parking lot, through the snow falling in thick clumps.

As soon as we arrived in the Day Surgery unit it was apparent that while non-elective surgeries would not be cancelled, elective ones could be. There were people sitting in the waiting room with overnight bags at their feet and phones at their ears trying to secure a ride back home or a hotel room for the night after receiving notice that their procedure had been delayed or outright cancelled. I pulled a number from the dispenser and took a seat to wait to check in, fully expecting to be told to head back home. At that moment, I'd have welcomed any excuse not to follow through with the surgery on that day. I imagined myself back at home on the couch with hot coffee and a roaring fire, watching the snow fall with my kids beside me.

I was holding a tray of homemade chocolate chip cookies for the staff of the Day Surgery unit in my lap as I waited, baked as a thank you for showing up despite the forecast. As I waited for my number to be called, I made a mental plan to simply drop the treats off and go home without accomplishing my surgical goals for that day, but I reasoned that at least I would've done something kind for the staff behind the admissions department doors.

My number was called and, to my surprise, the desk attendant checked the files in front of her and told me that all those necessary for my surgery were in attendance, everyone except me, that was. A nurse immediately led me through the locked door off the waiting room, through the hallways within, and to a bed with a chair beside it. Once again, I began preparing for the operating room.

First, I changed into the two-gown set-up that I was by then very familiar with. Next, I met the anesthesiology team and a few of the nurses who would be taking care of me throughout the roughly half-hour that the sedated portion of the surgical procedure would take. Then, my oncology surgeon came by to check in and trade comments on the forecasted weather.

"We'll get going soon and hopefully have a relatively uneventful surgical experience this time."

"Maybe we'll even be home before the snow accumulates," I responded, hopefully.

Within minutes of speaking with the surgeon, I was brought back to the operating room for my third round of anesthesia-induced time loss, and when I woke up a second later, just over an hour had passed. This reanimation was the first and only time I have been aware of being intubated. I woke up and opened my eyes while gagging, unable to clear the foreign object in my throat. It lasted for only a second or two before a nurse was beside me and suddenly I could breathe freely again.

I could hear voices and feel a warm hand on my arm. As I came fully to consciousness, I noticed the nurse next to me looking towards a colleague walking through the centre of the large recovery room and heard him announcing to the staff that a state of emergency had just been declared by the city of St. John's. Minutes later, we heard that many of the municipal councils of the surrounding communities had followed the same declaration in response to the volume and speed at which the snow was falling and blowing around outside. My surgery had been completed successfully, but I'd opened my eyes just as the doors to the hospital were closing to everyone.

I woke up slowly, slowly, and experienced the same sensation of a gentle but persistent current of nausea starting in my midsection and tumbling outward with growing ferocity. I was transported back to the post-surgical recovery area where Scott was waiting, and he updated me on the events that had transpired while I was nestled in the centre of the hospital having my lymph nodes removed. The wind speeds had picked up to near-hurricane strength, with sustained winds that bent power lines and broke off tree branches. This alone would not warrant a state of emergency, but when the wind was coupled with staggering amounts of snowfall it had essentially become a snow hurricane. At some points throughout the day, as I slept off my sedation on a gurney in the recovery ward of the hospital, upwards of ten centimetres of snow fell in a single hour.

The storm outside mirrored the storm that was building inside me and, by mid-day, I had been out of surgery for three hours and given up the hope that I would not be violently ill. Scott had gone to get coffee, and the nursing staff was doing a superhuman job of caring for the patients who had had surgery before the state of emergency was declared while also juggling all their new responsibilities as an emergent situation was unfolding outside the hospital. Because I could not physically manage to walk to a bathroom myself, and also because I had no idea where the bathroom was, I called out for help and immediately a nurse came to my side.

"Bathroom. Now," I managed to vocalize, and the combination of my words and my grey face conveyed the gravity of my need. The nurse produced a wheelchair out of thin air and, practically before I could blink, I was in a bathroom. This nurse parked the chair outside the door, lifted me up by my one unbandaged and unswollen armpit, walked me into the bathroom, and closed the door behind both of us. She held back my drain lines as the tsunami crashed on the shores of my body and I heaved again and again and again. Once I felt like I was done, she sat me on a chair that was in the bathroom and she washed my face with a cool cloth. She readjusted my gown and crouched on the floor beside me while I regained my focus, my lung capacity, and my dignity.

When I finally looked into her face, she smiled.

"Well, don't you look so much better now that you've gotten that over with!" she said with sincere joy.

Once I let go of my embarrassment, I realized that she was right. If there truly is power in knowledge, then I was now powerfully knowledgeable of the fact that I would be violently and deeply sick after being under anesthesia, but once it passed, I'd be fine once again.

Admittedly, I would rather not have this knowledge, nor have had additional opportunities to test the hypothesis.

CHAPTER THIRTY-TWO

Once again, I had a post-surgical drain in my body, although just one this time, and there were bandages wrapped across my chest. With the evacuation of my digestive system complete, the nurse wheeled me back to the gurney I had been transported from the operating room on and I slept deeply for hours. Every time I opened my eyelids and turned my head, Scott was beside me. It wasn't until the afternoon that I was consistently awake; however, once I had expelled the anaesthetic anger from my body and then slept for several hours, I seemed to be as fine as I could expect to be after having surgery—I was sore but alert. I expertly emptied my post-surgical drain, recorded the output, and then I was ready to get something to eat.

Scott helped me get dressed, an event that would be repeated constantly over the course of the next ten days. I was unable to independently lift my right arm away from my body by any significant distance, and it was far too soon for me to begin exercises to extend my range of motion.

Once I was out of the hospital gowns and back into my own clothing, I tucked my emptied drain into the pocket I'd sewn inside my shirt and turned to ask Scott where he wanted to go.

"To a window, that's for certain," he immediately replied.

"Where have you been outside of here?" I asked him. It had been hours since I'd been wheeled into the recovery space, and I had been sleeping for the majority of the time since I'd arrived. I assumed Scott had been out and back a few times since that one coffee run to see what the weather was like and assess how much time he'd need to clear the snow off our vehicle before we headed home.

"I haven't left," he answered.

In response to my shocked expression, he continued, "You think I would consider leaving just to go look out a window and come back to find you bleeding to death again? Not happening."

I was speechless. I assumed that I had slept through all the times he had left the surgery department to get food, to look outside, or to use the bathroom, because he was there every time I stirred. It wasn't that I had coincidentally seen Scott every time I opened my eyes and turned to look beside my bed, my sentry simply hadn't left.

"Have you talked to the kids?" I asked, refocusing to work the lump of love and gratitude out of my throat.

"Yeah, they're enjoying watching the snow but want to know when we're coming home."

"I want to know that too, actually."

"I've heard that it's pretty unreal outside. Some of the descriptions I've read online must be exaggerations. Dad says the driveway is totally filled in, but that's not that unusual. If I can get to our vehicle, I can get us home."

"It's time to go see for ourselves," I suggested.

Before we even had a chance to take a step towards leaving the unit, my surgeon appeared. He asked how I was feeling, listened when I explained that I had been intensely sick again, and then asked us if we knew that we wouldn't be going anywhere for the remainder of that day.

"I'm fine!" I began in protest.

"It's not about your recovery, it's the environment. Snow accumulation has already overwhelmed the roads. It's coming down at an unbelievable rate and with unbelievable wind behind it," he explained. "I'm not leaving the hospital either."

The post-surgical recovery room was situated in a unit at the very centre of the main floor of a five-storey hospital—we were located inside a massive concrete square without any windows. Scott and I had essentially been inside a bunker up until this point, which was why we both harboured a touch of skepticism that this storm was as historic as people were describing.

"If Ashleigh isn't medically required to stay here and I can get to my vehicle in the lot, we're going home," Scott said, looking at his watch. "It's barely three o'clock now, so there's plenty of time to get home before dark."

"I think you should go look outside," the surgeon replied. "I'm going to start the paperwork to have you admitted for the night. You'll at least have a room and a bed to sleep in instead of staying here in the recovery room."

All three of us looked around the large open room we were in, not vocalizing our thoughts but assessing the lack of privacy in the space that three other patients were also recovering in. There was also a noticeable lack of any surface that Scott could conceivably sleep on and only a single bathroom for each gender to be shared by all the patients, the people accompanying them, and the nurses working on the ward.

"Fuck," Scott and I said in unison.

We had still not seen the outside with our own eyes; however, my thoughts on storm severity were pushed aside by a sinking understanding that, not only would I not be in my own bed that night to keep Bean and Ava safe and snuggly as they fell asleep, Scott would not be either. This was not a possibility that we had planned for on any level. Scott and I headed out of the recovery unit and towards the front entrance of the hospital together.

In post-apocalyptic movies where the zombie illness has decimated the city and survivors are gathering in large buildings and discussing what they witnessed on the way there, sometimes there will be a hospital with patients milling around haphazardly in open-backed gowns with IV trees dragging behind them while someone is giving out food and water. That's the scene in which Scott and I found ourselves when we pushed open the doors of the Day Surgery unit and entered the general population of the hospital.

I had very limited mobility in my dominant arm and preferred to keep it pressed securely to my chest, and I was also mostly bald since my hair had barely grown past the stubble stage and I still didn't have eyebrows or eyelashes. In the movie scene of the huddled masses within the hospital, I was unequivocally one of the patients, just one without an IV tree wheeling along behind her (for once). As we walked through the main floor of the hospital, we learned from other patients that constabulary officers were positioned at the traffic lights at the entrance to the hospital parking lot, stopping anyone from making an attempt to leave the building via vehicle. We heard that forecasts now predicted seventy centimetres of snow may fall before the end of that day.

One of the few benefits of being a cancer patient is that you become very, very knowledgeable of the layout of the facilities in which you receive treatment. The Cancer Centre and the adult general hospital are on the same grounds and are connected by one hallway that I had become familiar with over the course of my many, many appointments. Scott and I made our way to the Cancer Centre, banking on the fact that few people from the non-staff population trapped in the hospital with us would know how to get there. My hunch proved correct, and Scott and I found ourselves standing in the Cancer Centre alone looking outside through floor-to-ceiling windows. For the first time since we had arrived that morning, we finally understood that the descriptions we had received throughout the day had indeed been very accurate—possibly even understated.

From our private vantage point, Scott and I could see the hospital maintenance staff clearing snow away from the doors and sidewalk in front of the hospital emergency department with a tractor. Snow was constantly moved from in front of the doorway by the bucket of a commercial tractor, but the snow was falling faster than the tractor could remove it. If I hadn't been watching this event as it happened, I would not have believed that snow could possibly fall so quickly or blow so furiously. Not only were we never getting to our vehicle to attempt to go home, we also couldn't even see the parking lot from less than four metres away at 3:15 p.m.

"At the very least, I figured you could go to the car and get me the blanket and bag of snacks," I said, staring at the enormous tractor pushing snow away from the emergency room doors and piling it up in the empty parking spaces and roads leading away from the hospital.

"The snacks!" he cried. "You had extra cookies in there!"

"Yep. Sandwiches, yogurt, and a bag of chips, too," I added.

"This is your fault. You told me not to bring the bags in," he said with an accusatory voice.

"I support the option to go get it," I told him.

"I can't even tell which direction the parking lot is in," he said, defeated. We were both resigned to being without sandwiches and cookies until we could get across the lot to retrieve them from our car.

This winter storm was quickly dubbed "Snowmageddon" in the media, and that name has held on for posterity. Before the end of this twenty-four-hour period, across the eastern coast of

Newfoundland, ninety centimetres of snow would accumulate, wind gusts would peak at over 170 km/h, and the capital city would be brought to a standstill by a legal state of emergency that would last for an entire week.

CHAPTER THIRTY-THREE

Recalling how my mastectomy hospital stay had run longer than planned when I was packing for this surgery, I had not only packed expecting to be admitted, but I had brought extra of everything I might need in case post-surgical complications kept me at the hospital for several days. I did not, however, at any point consider the possibility that my healthy husband would need to stay in the hospital for longer than the hours of surgery and recovery. We both assumed he would be able to go home to access such mundane items as his toothbrush, medications, and clean socks that same day. After a supper of hospital cafeteria pizza and fries, Scott and I made our way back to the Day Surgery unit to settle in for the night.

"I could use a stick of gum," Scott reported as we walked back to my gurney.

"Dream big, my love. Imagine having a toothbrush," I replied.

"I think we have found the limit to what I will share with you," he mused. "I will not use your toothbrush."

"I will not offer it, either," I agreed. "I mean, the last time I used it was after I barfed earlier, so I'm not sure *I* even want to use it again."

"Seriously, though. Where am I sleeping tonight?" he asked, knowing I did not have an answer. "You have the gurney—"

"Filled with my post-surgical sweat and farts."

"That no one in their right mind would wish to take off with," he concluded. "I'm not sleeping in the plastic chair I've been sitting in all afternoon. I'm also not thrilled about sleeping on the floor of an operating room recovery unit."

"You've never wanted to sleep in a petri dish?" I asked with a laugh.

"I'd feel better about it if I had those damned cookies to console me," he countered.

I have deep gratitude for the fact that my husband and I are best friends and can laugh at situations like this together until we are both legitimately crying.

While we were in the cafeteria, my surgeon had returned to the surgery department to inform us that we wouldn't be able to move to one of the hospital rooms after all. He wasn't the only doctor to try to get a patient admitted so they would have a more comfortable place to wait out the state of emergency, but by the time he submitted the request for me, all of the rooms in the entire hospital were occupied. The surgeon didn't find us in the unit, but he did inform the nursing staff of the development, and when we returned from the cafeteria we discovered that the nurses had found a convertible chair contraption for Scott to sleep on. He wedged it into the space between my gurney and the curtain that separated us from the patient recovering in the other corner of the open space. The nurses also found an unopened toothbrush for him and had even contacted the pharmacy in the hospital and ensured that he had the medication that he would have otherwise been unable to take that evening.

Scott and I finally lay down on our makeshift beds: me in a gurney meant to transport a patient from place to place before they're moved to an actual bed, and Scott on a vinyl-covered chair that claimed to convert to a bed but could only manage to recline backwards about twenty degrees farther than an average airplane seat. The place we were in was not designed with the idea of patients staying longer than a few hours, and certainly never for anyone bunking overnight. The fluorescent lighting overhead could either be on or off, with no dimming or even selective lighting options in between. The ten people who were attempting to rest in this large space peppered with obstacles—including medical paraphernalia, walls, doorways, and office furniture—could either exist in absolute pitch darkness or in tanning-bed brightness. Three of us had just undergone surgery that morning and each needed varying degrees of mobility assistance and monitoring overnight. Together we begrudgingly agreed that in this all-or-nothing fluorescent lighting scenario, we had to keep the lights on.

I wouldn't say I slept, really. My body did relax fractionally when Scott's mom texted us to say that both kids had fallen asleep with only minor upset. We had been in contact with Ava and Bean throughout the day, and both of my kids had demonstrated the grace, strength, and bravery that I can only hope to summon when faced with such a sudden and unexpected challenging situation. At some point, I did fall asleep because I was wrenched awake from that slumber after midnight when the hospital fire alarm began to wail. For twenty minutes, the sirens all throughout the Day Surgery unit, and by extension the entire hospital, cycled between ear-splitting wails, then a pre-recorded message asking us to remain calm, and then silence just long enough to be hopeful that it was over before it began anew. Fifteen minutes into this ordeal, with nowhere to escape the noise and no one to advise us on what the ever-loving hell was going on or when it might stop, I began to wonder if it was possible for us to dig our way out to our vehicle in the parking lot before the contents of my post-surgical drain began to freeze. Eventually, the sirens stopped and we all went back to laying in the brightness, staring at the ceiling and sweating—there wasn't any air conditioning in this particular unit either.

The next morning, the cafeteria initiated a tiered system of meal distribution where the hospital staff could get breakfast first, and then, during a pre-designated time, the patients and the people accompanying them could avail of a meal. This made the process of getting meals significantly faster and ensured that those who needed it most got fed first. The hospital staff in the building that weekend would work eighteen, thirty-six and, for some, as many as sixty hours straight before they were finally able to secure transportation home or be relieved by their colleagues. Give them the eggs and coffee first, please.

CHAPTER THIRTY-FOUR

Over breakfast on the day after Snowmageddon, Scott and I scrolled through social media and the local news sites taking in all the images bouncing around from the previous day and night. Four-lane highways were reduced to one single car width, plows travelled in tandem down major thoroughfares with snow reaching up to their windshields, and people's second-storey windows were stacked with snow right up to the very top. We lived a short twenty-minute drive from the hospital, but that morning it felt like we were a million miles from home. Fortunately, our house had not lost power once all night and Scott and I knew that our kids were out joyfully playing in the mountains of snow that blanketed our neighbourhood. I wanted to be there to play too, at least in whatever way my newly damaged body might allow.

Over the course of the day, we heard many rumours regarding how and when we would be allowed to travel on the roads again. At one point, I even added my name to a list of patients deemed healthy enough to be discharged, as there were talks of military escorts helping people get back to their homes. The state of emergency that had been enacted the previous morning meant that movement around the city and surrounding municipalities was legally limited to ensure emergency services vehicles could move quickly to wherever assistance was needed and so that the plows could continue the arduous work of moving snow again and again from every single street across the cities and towns. Several times, people had gotten stuck in their vehicles while out on the now significantly narrower roads, so there was significant motivation for people to stay off the streets for the time being. Scott and I would have been quite happy to stay home and off the roads—once we finally got there.

Lunchtime came and went with no updates on when we might be escorted home. In the late afternoon of this second day of confinement, Scott and I left the unit where we'd "slept" and went on a long walk around the hospital to discuss our options. Sitting in the chairs in the front of the Cancer Centre, and once again alone, we realized we could actually see our vehicle in the parking lot! It was a marked improvement from the previous afternoon when it had been undetectable behind a curtain of swirling snow.

"It's going to be dark soon," I said as we were sitting in the empty waiting room, watching maintenance workers clear snow from the footpaths and alcoves around the entrance of the hospital.

"I had the same thought," Scott replied, pensive eyes focused on the front entrance of the hospital.

"It doesn't seem as though anyone is going to tell us to go home."

"Of course not," he said, turning to look at me and away from the snow-blanketed parking lot outside the doors. "We aren't leaving here with the explicit blessing of anyone. It's too high of a liability to tell us outright that it's safe to leave," he reasoned.

"Did you hear the conversation happening by the coffee station? Someone was saying that there are fines of $1,000 being given on the spot to anyone caught driving on the roads without an essential reason."

"We won't be joyriding. We want to leave here and go straight home," he reminded me. "I'm not saying I won't enjoy the drive in all this snow, just that I won't go out of my way to be in it longer than necessary," he clarified with a smile.

"If we want to get home before dark, we'll have to choose to leave on our own or accept that we will be staying here for another night. I guess I need to be presumptuous and consider getting myself home after surgery to be an essential reason to be on the road."

We slipped into silence as we considered the options before us. Another night in the oven of the recovery ward, another night on a gurney that needed fresh linens, another night away from our kids.

"What if it's really, really bad and we get stuck somewhere? What if we have to spend the night in our vehicle somewhere between the hospital and home?" I asked. "Is the devil we know here in the hospital better than the one we don't stuck inside our car in a snowbank all night? I mean, I can't even help you shovel with my busted-up arm and drain full of bodily fluid."

"At least we'd have those cookies and sandwiches you made me leave in the car."

"Smartass," I said, with a sigh.

"I think we're doing this," he ignored my insult and instead kissed my worried face.

Scott had been checking in with the various traffic cameras available for public viewing all afternoon and felt he had a route plotted to get us home with the highest likelihood of open roadways. The snow accumulation on our street was impassable; however, we were the second house in and the main street in our neighbourhood was cleared. All my hesitation was finally overridden when my father-in-law told us that he was merely waiting on the word that we were heading out and he would be outside with our snowblower, clearing a pathway down our road to get our vehicle into the driveway. That was it, it was go time.

We went back to the Day Surgery unit and gathered our things. We left the hospital at five o'clock that evening and it took forty minutes to get from the parking lot to our neighbourhood, double the time it would take on an average day.

Meanwhile, my father-in-law had been outside clearing our street for no more than a few minutes before a neighbour came out to ask him what was going on. When he shared that his daughter-in-law was on the way home from the hospital after having had surgery the previous day, the neighbour contacted his friend down the street, and they all came outside with their own snow-clearing equipment to help. A third neighbour across the street suited up to help as well, and just before six o'clock that evening, the headlights of our vehicle swept across our street and illuminated four people pushing snowblowers down the middle of the road. The pathway to our driveway was not yet fully cleared for the width of our vehicle, but a walkway had been made ready for me, and I got out to walk into my home with tears in my eyes and gratitude in my heart. With Scott there too, the five people finished moving hundreds of pounds of snow out of the way, and less than half an hour after I walked through the door, Scott followed me in and collapsed on our bed with our kids. We were home without a monumental fine or a night spent stuck in a frigid car in a snow-bank, and with the knowledge that neighbours will come through when help is needed.

CHAPTER THIRTY-FIVE

Recovery from the removal of my lymph nodes continued to be very different from the recovery I experienced after my bilateral mastectomy. Perhaps it was due to the fact that the arm and shoulder move in so many more directions than the front of the chest, or perhaps it was the fact that I was dealing with the trauma of three surgeries in the same area over a mere six weeks—three times the scar tissue and three times the possibility of nerve damage. Whatever the reason, it took me longer to regain mobility in my dominant right arm and it also took nearly three weeks before my post-surgical medieval torture drain could be removed—over a week longer than before.

To this day, I struggle with the losses I have suffered as a result of having my axillary lymph nodes removed. I wear a compression sleeve when I am engaging in activities that require repeated muscle use in that arm. I also have to take precautions with my right hand and arm to keep my skin healthy and free of cuts. I wear rubber gloves when doing household chores and work gloves when doing literally anything outside with my hands. If I do get a cut on my right hand or arm, I strive to immediately clean it, apply antibacterial ointment, and bandage it quickly to keep out bacteria, otherwise it will begin to hurt within an hour. A paper cut on my right hand takes three times as long to heal as one on my left hand does in this body. On one occasion, a single fly bite to the upper part of my right arm caused swelling and radiated heat so significantly that it landed me in the emergency room followed by two weeks of antibiotics. Prior to my cancer diagnosis, I had begun a tattoo along my upper back that was meant to be extended down my right arm in future sessions, and now that can never be finished.

These limitations are not impediments to my ability to live after cancer, but taken together, they represent a small portion of the long-term effects cancer has had on my life. They are the necessary toll that I paid in order to receive the peace of mind that any potential cancer lying in wait inside my axillary lymph nodes could not continue onward and set up home in any other part of my body. The price has been steep, but I do not regret the transaction—though there are moments I continue to grieve deeply for the functionality of my body that I have sacrificed in order to continue onward.

Throughout the week that the state of emergency was in effect due to Snowmageddon, I focused on physical recovery and restarting my exercise regime to regain the use of my right arm. Once the snow had been pushed aside and cars could once again take to the streets, I began updating my friends and loved ones on the outcome of the surgery and how I was faring through recovery.

A few weeks after my lymph node surgery, I sent a few texts to my former high school classmate and fellow cancer-mate, Ashleigh, to let her know how my surgery had gone and to check in and see how her recent radiation regime had been going. After a few exchanges back and forth, I stopped hearing from her. I sent another check-in text at the end of January to say I was thinking about her and was always ready to listen if she needed to vent to someone who (almost) understood. Days after that text, I received the news that she had died. Ashleigh's metastatic breast cancer had spread too far and had taken over too many of her cells, and she passed a mere two years after her diagnosis. Scott was at work when I received the news of Ashleigh's death and, while I badly wanted to share this tragedy with him and by extension share my grief, I hesitated to call him.

Ashleigh and I had both had breast cancer and we both had kids nearly the same age, so I could see myself in her position so easily—a position of no longer being. Scott, however, would immediately identify with her husband. Ashleigh had left behind a partner and friend, and he faced the impossible mountain of grieving the loss of a person he'd expected to spend decades more with, while now raising their kids alone, and Scott had been only a cell's width from being in the same position for the past year. I spent the day with Ashleigh on my mind and her family in my heart, and they have not strayed far from that place since.

Mere hours after I learned of Ashleigh's passing, another cancer fighter put out a call for volunteers to stand in a kind of honour guard at Ashleigh's funeral. Cancer patients will sometimes gather at the funeral of a fighter who has completed their battle to offer a collective show of love, support, understanding, and anguish to rest beside the horror and grief that cancer brings to a funeral for anyone the disease takes. In Ashleigh's honour, a dozen breast cancer fighters gathered for her funeral, each wearing pink scarves and holding up a pink carnation at the entrance of her service in deference to the pain her family and friends were experiencing, and to recognize the grace and strength she embodied throughout her battle with the disease that all of us were so intimately affected by. I also wore socks that I'd made from fabric emblazoned with "Fuck Cancer." She had held this honour guard position for those who were taken by breast cancer before her, and now we assembled inside the doors of the gathering space to offer her life the same tribute. Because I had had my post-surgical drain removed just the day before the funeral and my body was still in recovery, I struggled to keep my carnation raised for the duration of the post-memorial procession. I know Ashleigh would not have cared if my performance was perfect but rather only that her honour guard was standing in its place around her family.

Having cancer as a young adult forces you to face mortality at a time when death is likely not something you consider to be visible on your horizon. Having cancer as a young adult turns you into a walking reminder to those of a similar age that they are also not immune to the possibility that a single diagnostic image could change their life in an instant. These realities of cancer diverged for me at Ashleigh's funeral because I was a living reminder of the possibility that cancer can strike at any age, and my dear friend a reminder that cancer takes indiscriminately. She could have been standing where I was, and it is by an unknowable turn of cellular divergence that our outcomes were not reversed.

Cancer gifts the receiver a burden that sometimes feels insurmountable, but within the burden the patient also receives clarity of purpose and clarity of importance. It is so very clear to me what is important in my life now that cancer has stripped away everything that is not. I am not grateful for the burden of cancer and will never wish this disease on any person; however, I am gradually learning how to be grateful for the things that the acid wash of living through cancer has uncovered for me. My friend and I reconnected only briefly before she was taken from all those who loved her, but cancer is the reason we reconnected and I am grateful for the brief friendship we shared.

In the vestibule immediately after the service, the attendees paused to console one another as we all gathered our winter layers. Because Ashleigh and I had initially met when we were teenagers going to the same high school, many of the people attending her tribute were former classmates I had not interacted with in any meaningful way in twenty years. I was just barely no longer fully bald, less than ninety days out from having both of my breasts removed, less than one month out from my latest surgery, and I'd had the drain from that surgery removed the day prior. I was, to put it kindly, less a hot mess and more an active dumpster fire. All these people my own age who also had young kids, marriages, and partnerships, who were establishing their careers, had come together to celebrate the life and mourn the loss of one of their own and, here I was, a corporeal manifestation of the disease that had taken her. To add even more discomfort to the situation, I was not then, nor had I at any point previously, been part of the inner social circle of these peers.

It quickly became evident that beelining it directly to the doors and out of the funeral home was the only path for me. As I made my way through the multi-generational crowd of people wiping tears and touching shoulders, I suddenly saw a face smiling and calling my name to beckon me over. It was Karen, the friend that I always seemed to run into after a major life event. Karen, who had danced and cried with me after hearing the news that my chemotherapy was proving effective against my breast cancer four months before. She pulled me into an embrace and then welcomed me into a circle of people all familiar to me from our shared teenage past.

It was clear that I was sick, it was clear that I was fighting too, and to the averted eyes and shocked faces I said hello and confirmed that I, too, had cancer. I briefly shared with the few people nearest to me that I had connected with Ashleigh literally on a hospital bed over the months that we shared space in the Cancer Centre and how grateful I was for her presence at the other end of my texts. It wasn't a long conversation, as it would have been inappropriate to centre myself and my fight on the day dedicated to recognizing the life and the achievements of our friend. The gaping hole left by the loss of my friendship with Ashleigh was nothing compared to the crevasse remaining within the hearts of these people, but she was important to me at a time when we both needed someone wearing similar shoes.

I left shortly after, feeling less like I had run from the space and more like I had honoured what my friend had given me in her last months by speaking of the gift of comfort she had provided to me with those who would grieve her loss every day for the remainder of their own lives. That happened only because of another act of kindness offered by a friendly face and a welcoming embrace. No dancing together this time, but no less a pivotal interaction between Karen and me all the same.

One week after I stood in vulgar socks with fellow fighters to honour Ashleigh's triumphs, I wore those same socks to meet with my oncology surgeon and receive yet another pathology report. Of the fourteen lymph nodes that he had removed in my second lymph node surgery, every single one had been sliced thin in the pathology meat slicer and examined in minute detail under a microscope, and no cancer cells had been discovered. Not a single cell.

PART FOUR

radiation therapy

We can complain because
rose bushes have thorns,
or rejoice because thorn bushes
have roses.

– ABRAHAM LINCOLN

CHAPTER THIRTY-SIX

Early in January, I'd had five small dots tattooed on my torso: two at the centre of my chest, two on my right side, and one on my left side during a radiation simulation. The tattoos were completed in the Cancer Centre by a radiation technologist and not in a tattoo shop, but the process of applying the markings was the same. Small prick of the skin with a needle, drops of ink pushed into the holes left behind, blood wiped off, left to scab and heal. Before the markings were added, the technologist positioned my body under an x-ray machine according to the treatment plan that my radiation oncologist had mapped out for my body. Once I was in the exact position I needed to lay in for the beam of radiation to strike my body in the right areas, the tattoos were made so that the exact position could be repeated day after day after day. The technologists administering my treatments would use these markers as a constant against which they would compare co-ordinates defined by the machine to line up my body. That's how precise radiation therapy is. The five tattoos act like a GPS, except there's never an update and I keep it forever. I would receive twenty-five radiation therapy treatments, one every Monday to Friday over the course of five weeks.

Radiation therapy is administered via the same type of x-ray machine that is used to image a broken bone—except in my case, instead of the x-ray imaging lasting milliseconds, I had to lay under the beam of intensely high-energy waves for minutes at a time. Radiation therapy is also quite boring, which was a welcome change from the turmoil and unknown of chemotherapy and surgery. While undergoing radiation therapy, I knew what to expect from my treatment every day that I went in. I knew the exact position I had to lie in on the slender metal table for the machine to properly target the spaces inside my body where cancer had grown so that the radiation waves might make the tissue in and around those spaces inhospitable for cancerous cells to multiply once again.

By the time I arrived for my first radiation therapy treatment, I had already checked in for medical appointments so many times that I had unintentionally memorized my twelve-digit provincial Medical Care Plan number. With routine sometimes comes comfort, and initially there was some ease when receiving radiation therapy; however, that ease would eventually give way to difficulty all the same.

Once my name was called and I left the waiting room of the radiation therapy department, it generally took less than twenty minutes from start to finish for one radiation treatment to be completed. For the initial week of treatments, I felt absolutely nothing. It seemed like I was taking two hours from my day, every day, to lay on a cold table in a hospital gown for twenty minutes for no demonstrable reason. There was no external evidence that I was fighting cancer in any way by showing up for all these appointments. The necessity to show up every day is one of the ways that radiation therapy was particularly disruptive for my family: it happened every single day and we had two young children who needed care. My husband could take a single day off for each of my chemotherapy treatments or a longer stretch of personal days after each surgery to take care of our kids and me, but he could not be absent from his job for five consecutive weeks. He also couldn't be absent for the varying amount of time each day that it took me to receive radiation treatments. Would I be in the waiting room for thirty minutes or two hours? I could never anticipate how long it would take for my name to be called. There are a lot of patients and machines to co-ordinate in the department, and I do not fault the staff for the unpredictable wait times; however, this meant that Scott wouldn't be able to know how long he'd have to stay home with our kids while I was at my appointments.

Over the course of the years that I have been a cancer patient, my kids have come with me to a myriad of appointments. They have sat in my lap as I've had blood drawn; they have accompanied me on check-ups with my lymphedema nurse; they have been at post-surgical appointments with my surgeon, and we've never encountered any concerns with or problems caused by their presence. If anything, they lowered my anxiety and their deepening knowledge of my treatments lessened some of their own fears. My kids are generally inquisitive and calm, and most often they contributed to the discussions I had with the medical professionals around me.

After all the steps we'd taken together as a family, radiation therapy was not a place they could accompany me. After the technologists positioned me on the sliding plank under the x-ray machine, they would leave the room and close a fifteen-centimetre-thick radiation-shielding door lined with lead. I would be alone in a room designed to contain the radiation waves that strayed from the machine I was under, and there was no way my children could be inside that room with me for these treatments, nor were they old enough to wait outside in the waiting room for the duration of a treatment. So, every single day for five weeks, Scott and I had to juggle child care—something that many families do for years. I am in awe of those families, because after two weeks, I was mentally exhausted.

When someone is receiving chemotherapy treatments or they undergo a major surgery, there is a measurable and visible deficiency in their life. If a friend with cancer is too sick to cook or clean, you drop off a meal or scrub a bathtub and you know you've contributed. I was physically very capable in the first weeks of radiation therapy, and yet without the support and unconditional availability of my dear friend Amy, I am not sure how I could have completed the schedule as set out by my radiation oncologist. Amy lived close to me at the time of my diagnosis and treatments and has a child aged right in between my two. Amy came to my home with her kid on some radiation therapy days, and she rearranged plans to be at her home on other days so my kids could be dropped off. On the days when Amy's life and plans could not accommodate taking on the responsibility of my kids too, Scott stayed home while I went to treatment, but those days were far, far fewer in number because Amy was there for all of us. I do not doubt for a moment that there were times that having my kids in her care every day was burdensome, and I do not begrudge her the kind swearing she may have lobbed in my direction during those times, but to her credit, Amy never once made me feel anything but supported and loved. It is my deepest wish that every young adult going through their own cancer hell has an Amy beside them.

In addition to the burden of child care, radiation therapy was also disruptive to my family due to the accumulated cost of driving back and forth to the Cancer Centre every day for five weeks. A few trips a month or even once a week at the height of my diagnostic imaging regime was my record for number of visits prior to radiation therapy, but now that I had to go back and forth every day, it didn't take long for the financial burden to become apparent. That gas cost would have been less had I been able to arrive at the Cancer

Centre and park quickly but no—oh no—first I'd have to navigate the parking lot in the middle of a Canadian winter where multiple parking spaces had been lost to snow mountains and where the outpatient cars, visitor cars, and in-patient cars all shared the same allotment of space. It wasn't uncommon for me to circle the parking lot for fifteen minutes before finding a space to park in. I was yelled at multiple times in that parking lot as I went to radiation therapy for the perceived violations of not vacating my parking spot fast enough, or for not scraping the snow and ice off my car with sufficient speed using an upper body that had just been blasted with radiation waves. Once, someone even honked at me because I was presumably taking too long to exit the lot as I said a sincere thank you to the lot attendant. On a few occasions, the parking lot was so overburdened, bursting with too many people needing to park and too few spots available, that I left and drove directly to Scott so he could return with me and drop me straight at the front doors. I was late on those days and often teary eyed with frustration over the lack of parking, lack of consideration, and lack of decency that I had to navigate in order to show up for my appointments. Human compassion and kindness wither and die in an overfull hospital parking lot.

Outside the specific difficulties of parking and child care, radiation therapy is generally a grind to accomplish every day. It's day after day of time away from regular life to complete a task that feels demonstrably less effective at eradicating cancer than other treatments. I understood its importance, but the payoff felt invisible compared to the dramatic effect that chemotherapy and surgery had on my carcinomas and body as a whole. I mused about this a lot, and my supportive friends heard me loud and clear. Some friends baked me treats, others loaned me books to read while I waited every day for my name to be called. A potter friend made me a custom coffee mug with "Fuck Cancer" emblazoned on the side; another friend embroidered the same phrase on a piece of broadcloth for me. After texting to check in on me one evening and hearing that I had a craving for her bread and butter pickles, a friend saw to it that two jars of those pickles were immediately delivered to my door by her husband.

My friends understood that I was physically tired and emotionally depleted from the constant requirements of cancer treatment and they responded with an outpouring of love that carried me forward on my hardest days. I have kept every single card that accompanied the gifts and meals that friends have given me, and they remain a tangible reminder that cancer is bullshit but that I am held up by many amazing people while I fight it. Among the myriad of lessons that cancer has taught me, the one that has been etched on my heart the strongest is that asking for help is not weakness and showing vulnerability results in those who care showing me their love. Love can be expressed with casseroles and freshly baked banana bread. I know this because I have dined on both.

CHAPTER THIRTY-SEVEN

By the third week of radiation therapy treatments, I developed a five-sided sunburn encompassing the whole right side of my chest where my breast had previously resided, with my mastectomy scar running roughly through the entre. As I finished more and more treatments, the pentagon on my chest darkened more and more, and eventually the skin split open and began to peel off, confirming why a pentagon is associated with demons. When starting radiation therapy, I was repeatedly warned against friction of any kind on or near the radiation site because the skin would begin to slough off as the treatments progressed, and if too much skin falls off in one area at once, or if it falls off early in the treatment schedule, then infection becomes a concern. It was impossible to prevent the skin covering my armpit from peeling away, and I developed large blisters that made it uncomfortable for my arm to touch the side of my body.

In addition to my daily microwaving, I also had other appointments at the Cancer Centre. On one such day, while driving in for a medical oncology appointment, I felt a sharp, painful pinching sensation under my right thigh as I was waiting at a traffic light. My initial thought was that something had poked me from inside my driver's seat, and I ran my hand under my thigh and across the seat edge as the light changed, but I found no sharp object under my leg. When I pulled my hand back and relaxed my leg onto the seat, I felt an intense sensation of focused, sharp pain and I instinctively knew that something had pierced through my jeans and into the flesh of my upper thigh. I yelped and reached under my leg again to feel for whatever was piercing my leg, and when I brought my hand back up there was a very large, very angry bee on my palm. Evidently, I had severely pissed it off with my initial hand squashing and it took that aggression out on my thigh when my body repeatedly invaded its personal bee space. When I looked down, the fuzzy little asshole was on my hand, buzzing loud enough for me to hear and twisting to try and stab my palm with its stupid bee butt. It was February in eastern Canada—just over a month after Snowmageddon—so where in the hell had the bee even come from!? I know that bees are responsible for so much of the food that I love and that we're meant to be sheltering and protecting them as a species, but in that moment, fuck. that. bee.

For some unknowable reason it made sense to me to close my hand around the bee and toss it, not out the driver's side window as I drove down the road but instead into the footwell of the vehicle. I was now driving towards the Cancer Centre amid four lanes of traffic with an angry bee somewhere in the footwell of my Subaru and a welt expanding on the underside of my right thigh.

Five minutes after tossing the stowaway to my feet, I pulled into the parking lot of the Cancer Centre, threw open my door, and jumped from the car. I immediately spotted the bee trying to wriggle under the panelling covering the centre console and I swore at it loudly. I literally said, "Fuck you, bee!" in the parking lot of the hospital. I could feel my leg pressing into the fabric of my pants as the welt swelled. I couldn't close the door and leave the bee inside my vehicle for fear it would use the time trapped inside to plot another attack on my body as I drove home after my appointment. I couldn't wait for it to decide to leave my vehicle on its own as I had an appointment to get to. I couldn't leave the window cracked as it was February and lightly snowing, plus I couldn't rely on the bee's ability to get out through an open window—what if it couldn't find its way out and I was back to the revenge-plotting scenario? In what was one of the most badass moments of my life, I reached into my car and scooped the bee up and tossed it once again, this time into the open air of the hospital parking lot. I danced on the spot for a few seconds and swore repeatedly before heading inside to check in for my appointment.

"Hi. I'm here for a medical oncology appointment," I said to the receptionist sitting behind the counter.

"All right!" she replied brightly, looking up to meet my gaze as she started typing on her keyboard. "Are you okay?" she asked, alarmed once she looked at me.

"Uhh. I just got stung by a bee?" I replied, questioning my own statement as I said it, despite just having lived the experience.

"What? Here?" She stood slightly and looked to the waiting room, perhaps thinking the bee was waiting patiently for its turn at registration.

"No, in my car. It was in my car," I reported, the disbelief fading with incredulity and hilarity taking its place. "Why was there a bee in my car in February, you ask? I DON'T KNOW! But it sure doesn't like me very much."

"A bee. In your car. In February," she summarized, also beginning to grin.

"And it stung me. Multiple times, actually. Can I have some ice?"

"This is a new one, even for this place," she said. She carried on checking me in for my appointment and quickly updated me. "All checked in. Best of luck with the leg and you head on downstairs to the Clinic B waiting area."

As she was giving me these instructions, she also handed me an empty plastic biohazard transport bag to fill with ice from the dispenser downstairs in the Cancer Centre.

"I'm sorry, where?" I asked, forcibly controlling the wobble of laughter in my voice as I took the biohazard bag from her outstretched hand. "Did you just tell me to head to 'Clinic Bee'?"

With that, we both abandoned any remaining shred of composure and laughed so hard that it made a thigh attack by a rogue bee during winter worth the pain. By the time I left the waiting room for Clinic B(ee), the attack zone on my thigh was soaked from the melting ice and so swollen I couldn't wait to change into the hospital gown, just so I could take my pants off.

CHAPTER THIRTY-EIGHT

Chatter picked up about two weeks into my radiation treatments regarding a virus sweeping the globe that was proving to be highly contagious and highly damaging to the human body, most especially to the immunocompromised. Over the course of two weeks of appointments at the Cancer Centre, the environment inside went from resigned and purposeful focus on the task of defeating cancer and supporting patients to one of balancing the need to continue striking back against cancer while also protecting the medically vulnerable. In early March of 2020, the COVID-19 virus was proving to be almost as random and vicious as cancer itself. Where previously cancer patients were not only allowed but openly encouraged to bring support people along with them to their appointments, they were now largely forced to go it alone for their own safety as well as the safety of the patients around them. The medical staff remained unfailingly kind and, if anything, took even more care to support those receiving treatments; however, they also had a job to carry out and could not sit with a patient for hours to support them in the same way a friend or family member could. Being an active cancer patient during the beginning of an outbreak of a highly contagious and life-threatening virus was an impossibly lonely section of a road that was already hellish and isolating.

The radiation therapy waiting rooms had previously been a place where a dozen or more patients waited for treatment appointments, often with a partner or friend staying in the room while the patient went behind the concrete door. In the first weeks after the world began to comprehend the gravity of COVID-19, the waiting rooms turned from places of connection to rooms deserted of people, with fear filling the vacuum left by their absence.

The positioning of breast cancer radiation therapy means that the lung cannot be avoided in the pathway of the radiation beam. I was told that I should be mindful of the possibility of compromised lung functionality while receiving radiation therapy treatments to my chest, but also at any point thereafter. I was twelve treatments into my twenty-five treatment radiation plan when the World Health Organization declared a global pandemic due to COVID-19. I was halfway through a cancer treatment plan designed to ensure that the parts of my body that had allowed cancer to grow previously were made unwelcome for cancer to reside in again, a side effect of which was potentially compromised function of my right lung, while a highly transmissible virus that caused massive respiratory impacts was barreling across the globe. Between the options of stopping radiation therapy to isolate at home and avoid the potential of being inadvertently exposed to COVID-19 while in and around the hospital versus continuing the radiation therapy to lessen the possibility of a cancer recurrence, I chose the devil I knew as the foe I wished to vanquish. I continued onward, day by day, taking one more bite of the cancer elephant, this time with radioactive teeth.

CHAPTER THIRTY-NINE

Each Monday when I arrived for my radiation therapy appointment, the receptionist at the front desk of the Cancer Centre would check me in and hand me a printed schedule of all my appointments for that week. I'd immediately co-ordinate child care with Amy and Scott and I'd add five more lines to my radiation therapy tally. On Monday, March 23rd, 2020, I received two printouts instead of one. The second one had just one date and one notation on it: March 30th: Final Radiation Therapy. I could see the finish line in the distance, and it was what kept me moving forward that final week.

The skin that used to cover my underarm area had fucked off and given up days ago, leaving my armpit and triceps areas light pink and raw. The worst part about attending radiation therapy at this late stage in treatments was the necessity for me to put on a shirt to leave the house, as the friction caused by even a single layer of cotton would at times make my eyes water. I was well past the ability for any type of over-the-counter ointment or cream to provide any relief and, by my final week of microwaving, I was using a prescription cream called Flamazine® multiple times a day. The fact that the prescription cream used on severe burns is called Flamazine is a level of pharmacological trolling that is quite simply unparalleled.

Monday, March 30th, couldn't come soon enough. After my final radiation appointment, I could stay home with my family and shelter in place properly while also recovering from the blistering cancer prevention treatment. Two days before my final treatment, Becca called from Ontario. Word was spreading across social media that Karen—our high school companion and the friend who had danced with me to celebrate positive treatment results and folded me in inclusion after saying goodbye to a woman far too young—was gone. Unbelievable at first, then quickly confirmed as true, Karen's unexpected death highlighted the depths of what we did not know about each other's lives. My life and thoughts had been fully focused on fighting cancer and grieving the loss of friends who also had some version of the same disease that I had. Karen's death was a gut-wrenching reminder that young lives are lost without any involvement of cancer.

Two days after I learned about Karen's death, I rang that iconic and pivotal end-of-treatment bell in the Cancer Centre. I thought of Karen as I changed out of a hospital gown and into my own clothing for the final time, and of how she likely would have revelled in the accomplishment of that moment. I thought of the unabashed joy she would have shared with me if I could have told her about this day, shown her a video of the occasion the next time I ran into her, how we could have danced furiously behind the cash register lineup again.

Many of the radiation technologists who had moved me centimetre by centimetre into the correct positions over the course of the previous five weeks accompanied me upstairs to the main entrance of the Cancer Centre after I'd changed out of my radiation garments. Prior to the beginning of the COVID-19 pandemic, there had been a large brass bell next to the main elevator bank that patients could ring at the end of any, or all, of their personally defined milestones along their treatment path. That bell was now gone because few scenarios would be more tragic than a person ringing that bell to signify the end of one of the most difficult roads in their life only to contract COVID-19 from joyous contact with the symbol of their triumph. Instead, I pulled out my phone and opened the bell app that I had installed for just this exact moment. Surrounded by a dozen people, a combination of the Cancer Centre staff who had supported me and knew I was marking a milestone, as well as some patients who shared this joy with me merely by happenstance, I rang the shit outta that bell on my phone while I stomped, danced, and waved at my husband and two kids watching from outside. COVID-19 robbed me of the ability to share this monumental moment with my family inside the building, but they were still there watching.

In the weeks that would follow that day, I developed a serious infection deep within my radiation field that demanded two courses of antibiotics and a metric tonne of acetaminophen before it left my body. My skin grew darker and shrivelled across my mastectomy scars, much of it sloughing off to reveal blisters, which would eventually give way to new, pink skin. Just like chemotherapy, I had more recovery ahead of me after leaving the Cancer Centre, but on the happy day that I rang that bell-impersonation app and then physically-distance-hugged the people around me, I had finally collected all my tally marks for radiation therapy treatments.

I literally ran outside the main doors of the Cancer Centre and into the embrace of my best friend and our daughters so we could all go home.

One bite at a time.

PART FIVE

living

Life is not a having and a getting,
but a being and a becoming.

– MYRNA LOY

CHAPTER FORTY

Months after completing treatment, I was cleaning unnecessary medications out of a cupboard in my home and I found two bottles of antinausea medications pushed to the back. Just the sight of the names of those medications in my house caused a tailspin into panic and fear. My breath got shallow, my skin prickled, I lost all sense of time, and felt that I was back in those post-chemotherapy days needing those medications every four hours on the clock to be able to survive the day. This is what survivorship looks like for me, and there is a version of this held by the body and the mind of every cancer patient who rings a bell and then attempts to move forward. As I move through my life and discuss my experience with cancer, I sometimes say that I have cancer in the present tense and not that I *had* cancer in the past tense. As far as I can be aware, there are no cells dividing uncontrollably within the confines of my skin at this moment, and yet I live every single day with the collateral damage of having had cancer. To look at me today, someone might realize that my chest expanse is concave, but my hair has now grown back and I otherwise appear to be an average middle-aged female-presenting person. Inside my body, however, with the absence of all the lymph nodes in my right arm, plus the accumulation of three surgeries' worth of damage to my chest and arm, my body does not function like that of an average person. I should never sit in a hot tub or a sauna because of the risk that the intense heat could cause lasting swelling in my arm, and a similar situation applies to flying in an airplane. Certainly, people with less effective lymphatic systems fly all the time, but the activity does necessitate the use of compression garments for the duration of a flight and for hours afterwards. My body is free of cancer, but the magnitude of damage left behind is why I often feel it is imprecise to say I "had" cancer, to suggest it is behind me. My body, my life, is not free of the shock waves.

There is also the psychological trauma that cancer leaves in its wake. At some point after chemotherapy finished and before radiation began, I learned that I should consider accepting a biannual IV infusion of a bisphosphonate medication that reduces the possibility of a cancer recurrence in my bones. Chemotherapy can be treacherous on the bones, and the bisphosphonate can help to lessen the breakdown of bone tissue after chemotherapy is finished, while also reducing the chance of bone cancer metastasis. With minimal significant downsides, I agreed to the medication; however, because it is administered via an IV, it means that I have to return not just to the Cancer Centre, but into the very belly of my PTSD beast—the chemotherapy unit—to receive the treatment.

For all the days that I have returned to the Cancer Centre after finishing chemotherapy treatment, I have struggled to even look at the waiting room to the suite where chemotherapy is administered. Yet, twice each year, I sit back in the reclining chairs, smell the hospital disinfectant in the recirculated air, and look at the pictures on the walls in the open room in which I repeatedly endured the worst experiences of my entire life. The physical and psychological endurance needed to drag my broken body across the finish line of my sixth cycle of chemo left an imprint on my life that has not diminished with time, and going back into that room twice a year for an appointment with a medication that might aid me in never needing to come back for chemotherapy is difficult to reconcile. The post-traumatic stress that I experience whenever I am reminded of the smell, taste, or feel of chemotherapy is why I have cancer in the present tense.

In addition to this biannual IV infusion, for two years I took medications that suppressed the estrogen my body produces. After finishing chemotherapy, I began a monthly injection administered via a needle plunged into the skin of my stomach that deposited a small rod into my flesh to slowly release a hormone-suppressing medication. The suppression prevented my body from ovulating, stopping the influx of estrogen and progesterone that ovulation brings. This ovulation suppression was kept constant by repeating the injection every twenty-eight days for fourteen consecutive months. For many days throughout those fourteen months, I struggled to regulate many aspects of my life affected by the premature menopause the implant caused, but it was the effects of the daily oral hormone therapy medications I also took that made the changes insufferable. My ovaries, the powerhouse estrogen producers of the body, were fully suppressed by the monthly injection, and the daily pill stopped the production of small amounts of estrogen by all of my other organs. While on hormone therapy, I suffered debilitating hot flushes daily, sometimes hourly. I suffered from wild swings in patience and mood that exhausted me emotionally in my quest to control and regulate my mental state. I also suffered from a variety of discomforting complications affecting my uterus and endometrial lining, and I had pain in my joints and bones that made physical movement difficult every single day.

After two years and many, many conversations with my husband, my medical oncologist, and with myself, I made the difficult decision to end daily hormone therapy. The scales in my quality of life had finally tipped too far away from positive when I began to wonder if my kids would be better off attending public school instead of being homeschooled by a mom who was constantly losing her temper, crying at the slightest complication, physically unable to take them on adventures outside, and generally wasn't enjoying the life we'd so consciously chosen. I decided that the risk of cancer recurrence was worth it in my situation if the trade-off was regaining my ability to feel joy, control anger, and sit through sadness, believing that calm would come once again. Staying on hormone therapy wasn't the right choice and yet stopping it didn't feel like the right choice either because both are awful decisions to be set in front of a young cancer patient. One path involved taking a treatment that was debilitating and the other path involved opting out of that treatment and accepting that I'd have a higher possibility of cancer recurrence. There is no right here, there is only less awful, and my choice was to prioritize my quality of life.

CHAPTER FORTY-ONE

"Now that all the cancer stuff is behind you, I bet you can't wait to get back to normal!"

"What! You can't have cancer that bad, you look so good!"

Allow for some variations within these comments and you can multiply by the dozen to calculate how many times I've heard each. Once I rang the bell, I experienced so many well-intended iterations of enthusiasm at the idea that I could "go back to normal," but that suggestion utterly ignores the fact that I was not the same person I had been before my diagnosis and, therefore, even if my previous life still existed, I would no longer fit into that life in the same way—there was no going "back."

There is an equal sharpness to comments meant to compliment me on the visually undetectable status of my disease, and I do understand that these types of observations are born of a deep desire by the speaker to believe that their friend or loved one is going to survive. A deep desire to disassociate this unwell person from the vibrant or strong or present person that they knew before cancer invaded their entire being and smashed up the place. Yet, my recovering body and all of its former selves are vessels for the same person, so saying I can "go back to normal" or "but you look so good" leaves no room for the growth that inevitably has to occur when any person comes through a terrible experience. For me personally, suggesting I am about to go back to normal as I near the finish line on any cancer intervention leaves no ability for me to completely accept the fact that my previous priorities and life are now gone. It leaves me no ability to be okay with where I am now.

Yet, where am I now?

"Why do I bristle whenever someone lobs the phrase 'back to normal' at me?" I asked Scott one day during the summer after my final radiation treatment.

"Because finishing active treatment is not a doorway you walk through and then it's behind you," he immediately replied. "There is no switch that can be flipped in order to forget what you've been through physically or emotionally."

"Right. I can't un-see how fragile life is. I can't leave the hospital for the final time and leave my understanding of mortality behind as well," I said, processing these thoughts as I was speaking the words. "So, then, why is the phrase 'back to a new normal' somehow even worse?" I asked, laughing.

"Because sometimes it feels like nothing will ever feel normal in any way again," he replied.

It isn't easy to tease apart why a well-meaning comment can stick like a thorn in the side. Just as the conversations around diagnostics and staging were best had with fellow patients, conversations about what it is to be a changed person after cancer treatment are often most cathartic when engaging with fellow survivors. To be accepting of the fact that my life and my body are both vastly different now is not a rejection of everyone who was a pillar of my previous life, but it can feel that way to those who have not gained the perspective that cancer shoves down the throat of the patient. This is why I would never be able to accomplish the hard work of facing my emotional instability or processing my frustration towards those in my life who just cannot understand what it is to be a cancer patient, without the network of fellow young cancer patients that I have.

Living with and after cancer requires people who fully understand the daily physical and emotional struggles set in front of the person who is trying to build a life again from the bits left in the aftermath. It does not mean that the friends I had before cancer are not important to my healing, it simply means that I have newly added needs as I assemble my life with cancer that can best be understood by others who have had those same hurdles in front of them. It is impossible to explain how the trauma response of smelling the same cleaning solution used in the chemotherapy unit while shopping in a retail store three years after I completed chemotherapy can be so severe that I sprint to the exit; however, I don't need to explain that to the women I've met in the beds beside me. They know that smell and that trauma response, too.

The physical and emotional scars I live with are real, whether they are visible on the outside or not. I am different physically, emotionally, in personality, in the choices I make, and it's okay to acknowledge that. I feel more validation as a survivor and a thriver when someone recognizes how I am changed instead of assuming that I will be fully well only when I look and act like I did prior to having cancer.

After completing my final treatment, I had physical healing ahead of me, yes, but I had emotional healing to tackle as well. The emotional recovery needed after each and every treatment intervention can be pushed ahead and ahead comparatively easily while you are focusing on the very tangible work of trying to survive another day, another week, when going through active treatment. Once I'd finished that last radiation therapy treatment and rang the bell, I did not have a calendar full of appointments to manage anymore; however, I did have the wreckage of my life to make sense of, and that life looked almost nothing like it had before cancer. You can only push that emotional recovery ahead so far before it pushes back and demands to be examined, reconciled, unpacked.

"Maybe that's really it," I said to Scott after a long stretch of silence. "Suggestions of going back to normal after living through a major cancer intervention ignore the road that I have come down by assuming that I even want to go back to the place I was when I started."

"It's like that phrase you wrote beside the bed," he said, "'Recovery is Not Linear.' Maybe recovery also means not trying to get back to where you were when you started. You don't need to 'go back' to be 'normal.'"

As I reassemble a life with my husband and kids, it's all right if I have days where my arm just won't co-operate with my plans and requires me to modify an activity because I cannot depend on physical strength. It does not mean that the way my body functions in this moment is the way it will always be. Likewise, if I go days or weeks without wondering if cancer is seeping into my bones or brain and then I spend a whole night staring at the ceiling, fearful of a recurrence, it does not mean that I will be this way for forever. No recovery from a major life event is ever linear but rather has an ebb and flow, and it is within this stretching, relaxing, and regressing that we build the muscles—the resilience—to carry onward.

PART SIX

surgery (again)

You don't know how strong you are,
until your sole choice is to be strong.

CHAPTER FORTY-TWO

During the peak of cancer appointment haze, a health care worker asked me if it would be all right to share my contact information with a representative from the RuBY study. I said yes and promptly forgot about their request. As it turns out, the RuBY study is a national research initiative that is focused on "Reducing the bUrden of Breast cancer in Young women" and is funded jointly by the Canadian Breast Cancer Foundation and the Canadian Institutes of Health Research. They contacted me to see if I would be interested in participating in a long-term study of women under forty with breast cancer. The study consisted of a primary research project as well as many other sub-studies with narrower focuses under the umbrella of breast cancer.

Many months later, after I had completed radiation therapy, I received a call from one of the RuBY sub-studies that I had opted to participate in. For this sub-study, I'd consented to have my genetic profile mapped, then anonymized, and included in a dataset with other women diagnosed with breast cancer prior to turning forty. The study researchers would then use the data to look for patterns between gene differentiations and a variety of cancer types. In exchange for that anonymous participation, I received genetic profiling significantly faster than I would have been able to access it through a general referral to a provincially funded genetic counsellor. The phone call I received from the research group was to let me know that my profiling had been completed and that an anomaly had been discovered in the blood samples that they processed.

"This is unexpected," I began the conversation. I was immediately thinking about my two kids and how this finding may affect them in the future. "Is it BRCA?"

"BRCA1 and BRCA2 are two of the genetic factors that were part of your screening, yes; however, those cancer-suppressing genes were not identified as mutated. They were not contributing factors in your breast cancer," the RuBy representative reassured me. "I can tell you have some knowledge of genetics and the possible contributing factor of anomalies in cancer presentation."

"I also have two daughters," I confided.

"Let's not dance around this finding then. Ashleigh, you carry a CHEK2 genetic anomaly within your DNA. Ongoing scientific research has determined that there is a correlation between this anomaly and certain types of cancer—breast cancer being one. While it's possible that your kids have the same anomaly that you do, it does not mean that they're at a substantially higher risk of developing cancer—it means there's a medium risk of that happening. Now that you are aware of the presence of this genetic change, you and your kids can take steps to screen for the cancers the mutation is correlated with at the appropriate times," she explained. "Additionally, it is entirely possible that they're not even carriers of the mutation. It is not a given that children of a carrier have the same mutation."

"Okay," I paused to absorb. "Can you tell me the name of the mutation again?" I asked.

"Absolutely. CHEK, spelled like C-H-E-K, and then the number 2. There are a few variations of the CHEK2 mutation but they all function, or perhaps it's better to say malfunction, in the same way," she carried on. I was listening while also logging into my library account so I could search the catalogue for books on genetics and genetic mutations.

"DNA is complex and entire books have been written about a single genetic anomaly. The CHEK2 mutation is thought to shut down some part of the body's natural ability to recognize and then remove cancer cells in their very early days. It does not mean that everyone that has a CHEK2 anomaly will develop breast cancer, nor does it mean that every young person that already has breast cancer also has this sequencing error."

"You said there are other cancers it may be unable to recognize. What other kinds?" I asked.

"Breast, ovarian, fallopian, and colorectal are the four areas most closely associated with cancer development in patients that are identified as also having the CHEK2 variant. This mutation carries only a moderate correlation with cancer, which further means that there are many, many people that carry it and have no idea nor likely ever will."

"So, CHEK2 is not the reason I have cancer specifically, but it probably didn't help."

"I think that's a fair statement to make. Having a CHEK2 anomaly is one more piece to add to your own cancer puzzle, but it's still a piece that cannot be left out," she responded.

"What do I do with this information now? Do my kids need to be tested for it?" I asked.

"No. There is no known correlation between CHEK2 and any pediatric cancers, so testing your kids would actually be highly discouraged. It does not add any benefit to knowing at a young age whether they are carriers. If they decide to pursue testing in adulthood, it would ideally be carried out in much the same way yours has been, with a genetic counsellor discussing the results and screening suggestions with them based on their own results."

"I have to admit, I feel unmoored by this information. I know cancer at my age is uncommon, but I don't think I believed it would be a result of a genetic mutation."

"That's perfectly understandable. As I said, genetics and DNA are complex and you are learning about the very surface while hearing that your own DNA has an anomaly. It's a lot to digest."

"That feels like an accurate way to put it," I confirmed.

"Let's get to some of the positive aspects of having this information. CHEK2 does not seem to impact the body's ability to identify cancer cells altogether, but rather just cancer cells in those organs we discussed—breast, ovary, fallopian tubes, and the colorectal system. Also the testicles for male carriers. This is unique knowledge that points to specific organs that should be screened either more often or earlier than the average guidelines recommend," she concluded.

"This info certainly would have been good to have before I knew I had breast cancer," I said.

"Exactly. You do, however, have the information now and for all the days ahead of you," she gently reminded me.

"So then, if I was diagnosed with ovarian, fallopian, or colorectal cancer in the future, it would not be a stage 4 metastatic version of the cancer that I already had but a new cancer altogether?"

"That's an excellent conversation to have with your oncologist, since I do not have access to see your full medical file. I will say that if cancer cells developed in your breast and were not identified because of the CHEK2 gene, and later cancer cells developed in your ovaries, fallopian tubes, or colon and those cells were also not identified because of the CHEK2 malfunction, then that would be a second diagnosis of primary cancer and not a metastatic diagnosis of breast cancer. Does that make sense?"

"Mostly, yes," I laughed. "Cancer born not from a collection of travelling breast cancer cells but instead from another event of rapidly dividing cells that my immune defenses did not identify as hazardous and remove."

"Yes," she confirmed immediately. "It also means that your medical team knows where cancer is most likely to begin anew within your body and they can now check those places long before suspicious symptoms arise."

Knowledge replaces fear, I think, once again.

The presence of the CHEK2 anomaly would later be confirmed by another DNA-typing test completed by the RuBY study clinicians, and then confirmed yet again by a blood test carried out at the province's genetics research centre. Now that I know more, I do more by screening for cancer in the places where my genetic malfunction could prevent my body from identifying it. This genetic information factored into my surgery decisions and is the reason that I had my first colonoscopy at age thirty-seven.

I will forever bow at the altar of science.

CHAPTER FORTY-THREE

From the very first discussion of treatment possibilities, I knew that I would eventually need to consider the benefits versus risks of a full surgical removal of my ovaries—an oophorectomy. Chemotherapy claimed my ovulation as a casualty in the quest for cancer dominance because my ovaries perceived my body as unable to support life and so they stopped releasing an egg. Even though I was thirty-five when I finished chemotherapy, it remained possible that I would regain fertility and begin ovulating regularly again after the treatments concluded. I was not yet close enough to the average age of natural menopause to be confident that my ovaries would simply acquiesce to the onslaught of chemotherapy and retire. Plenty of people with breast cancer have gone on to have biological children after treatment concludes, some using eggs frozen prior to chemotherapy and others via standard conception methods once fertility returns.

"Have you come to any decision on the oophorectomy?" my medical oncologist asked me at the end of a routine appointment. It was early spring and I was still at the beginning of my twenty-five radiation therapy treatments, the final segment of the "active" stage of my cancer treatment.

Physical exam complete, I shed the hospital gown and pulled on my T-shirt as we continued talking.

"That's the surgery to remove my ovaries, right?" I asked as I reached behind the curtain and tossed the gown into the hamper for dirty linens and then rinsed and dried my hands in the small sink beside the examination table. I knew this place and the many rooms nearly identical to it very well after the hours I'd spent within them waiting for doctors and treatments.

Exam and waiting rooms offer a physical space perfectly appointed for the wandering mind to probe all the existential questions that facing mortality brings up. I'd used the time spent in waiting rooms and on examination tables to consider how far I was willing to go to prevent cancer recurrence. I'd sat in the chemotherapy unit for hours and wondered when the very first cell divided too rapidly inside my body. All bodies contain rapidly dividing cells, and all bodies also create cancer cells, but at what point in my body's history did it lose the ability to identify, isolate, and evict an errant cell? Could anybody tell me unequivocally and honestly that there was not a single cell of cancer in my body at any moment? Of course not. What if one little fucker jumped ship from my lymph nodes before they were removed and took up residence in my liver or bones but had yet to convince any of its neighbouring healthy cells to divide, divide, divide? No diagnostic scan can view the body externally at such a scale as to see a single cell, so the fact remained that cancer elsewhere in my body would not be discovered until it either grew to such a size that it created a visible carcinoma or caused side effects suspicious enough to warrant investigation.

Many hours of philosophical waiting room thoughts brought me to the conclusion that since breast cancer cells could exist inside my body even without any breasts on my body at all, there was nothing preventing those cells from blossoming into cancer once again. I'd imagine facing secondary breast cancer in another organ of my body *after* a bilateral mastectomy, because that does happen. If that cell was floating around in my body looking for the perfect environment in which to expand, I did not want my ovaries around feeding it the hormones it grew so exquisitely in the company of. It was the decision I took the most time to come to of all my major treatment options, but once again I decided on the path that would most fully remove any possibility that this cancer could find a foothold in an estrogen-rich environment inside my body.

"Yeah, I'm going to have them removed," I told her. "The genetic stuff was really the deciding factor, though I was pretty sure I was going to do it even before I found out about CHEK2."

"It's not an easy decision to make, but it is definitely something that should be thoughtfully considered in the case of estrogen-positive cancer," she confirmed.

"It will be nice to stop receiving the ovulation-suppressing injection, I'm sure," she continued. "It isn't comfortable to receive."

"It's not the greatest experience," I confirmed. "They don't want me to self-administer this one because the needle is basically the same gauge as a ballpoint pen, so I go to the community health clinic every four weeks. Plus, it's $100 out of pocket, even with my insurance covering the majority of the cost," I added.

"All right, I'll send a referral to one of the gynecologists that performs this surgery," she said as she made a note on my chart. "It'll be a bilateral-oophorectomy since both ovaries are removed in the procedure. I don't expect it will take too long to hear back on an initial consultation appointment."

"I think I need a few months," I took a deep breath and steadied my breathing. Just thinking about surgery quickened my heart.

Another operating room.

Another expanse of lost time while under anesthesia.

Another recovery with violent retching after waking up.

"I need to recuperate, you know? After my experience with the mastectomy, then the bleed, and then the lymph node dissection all within two months—I need to move farther away from the surgical experiences I've just had before this one is scheduled." I looked down at my lap and was surprised to see my hands quaking.

"Absolutely, Ashleigh," my medical oncologist replied quickly and softly. "I'll send the referral and if you're not ready for a consult when they call, that will be perfectly all right."

Ultimately, the surgical removal of my ovaries was not considered mandatory for long-term survival. My own Pros/Cons dichotomy came down to the "Pro" of long-term peace of mind in knowing that I had done everything tolerable and manageable to prevent cancer from recurring at any point in my future. In the context of a body that could conceivably continue to be fertile for fifteen years or more, the repeated twenty-eight-day injection is a burden. Freedom from the medical tether of having to get an injection every four weeks was not inconsequential, but there was no harm in waiting a few months. The bonus of not spending $100 every month also could not be ignored.

It was meant to be just a few months of pause to recuperate in which I would continue to receive the injection every twenty-eight days, except COVID-19 reared its unruly head and unleashed a clusterfuck of backlogs across the whole health care system less than one month after I confirmed my decision with my medical oncologist. My first consultation with a gynecological surgeon was scheduled and quickly cancelled because my surgery was not for cancer resection but for prevention. Medical supplies were scarce across the country and all non-essential surgeries were put on pause until supply-chain shortages could be addressed. Additionally, most gynecological surgeons are also obstetricians, and while cancer waits for no one, it can be quelled with things like an injection, whereas babies are coming when they're ready, no matter what the outside world would prefer. It was nine months after my axillary lymph node surgery before I saw a gynecological surgeon in person for the first time regarding the removal of my ovaries.

CHAPTER FORTY-FOUR

The first surgical consult appointment I had was in the fall of 2020, eleven months after I'd had my bilateral mastectomy. This consultation happened with a doctor who could schedule me in for the procedure in less than two weeks. I was surprised and excited to have this over and done with so soon after the initial appointment. When discussing the procedure itself, I specified that I would like my ovaries as well as my fallopian tubes removed because of the known correlation between a CHEK2 mutation and cancers in both reproductive parts. As it turns out, removing the section of each of the fallopian tubes that is outside of the cervix and that leads to the ovaries is standard in this situation, so the surgery I would be having was a bilateral salpingo-oophorectomy. After discussing the procedure and what recovery would look like, I left the office with a date for my next major bodily modification.

My ovary removal was the first surgery that I would be undertaking post-COVID-19 outbreak, and that meant that this time my pre-admission procedure would not resemble what I had undergone for my mastectomy or lymph node removal. In addition to a greatly reduced number of patients in the pre-admission clinic, I would also be required to have a molecular COVID-19 test prior to surgery and to isolate at home from the time of sample collection until my surgery. My pre-admission appointment was scheduled for a Tuesday and my COVID-19 test the next day, on Wednesday, in anticipation of my surgery on Thursday.

In the middle of the week before surgery, as I was preparing for another post-surgical recovery period, I woke up with a sore throat and mild congestion. I ignored it for the morning but by mid-day it was clear that I was coming down with a cold; however, I thought that with rest and fluids, I might be able to kick it during the full week I still had before my oophorectomy. By Monday of the following week, I was still congested, and I called the pre-admission office to seek their advice on what to do.

"I've been congested since Thursday of last week," I explained to the man on the other end of the phone.

"When is your pre-admission appointment?" he asked.

"Tomorrow," I replied.

"You can't enter the hospital with any symptoms of COVID unless you have produced a negative test in the previous twenty-four hours," he explained. "Have you already had your pre-admission swab?"

"The swab is Wednesday, but even if that's negative, I can't come in after that because I'm supposed to isolate after the swabbing," I reminded him.

"Right," he replied slowly. He was clearly doing the same mental gymnastics I had been engaged in all morning trying to figure out how to isolate and also go to the hospital for my pre-admission appointment after my COVID-19 test was completed. "There's really no way to line this up without you getting two COVID swabs unfortunately, and even then, you might be too congested for anesthesia to approve your surgery."

"Crap," I summarized.

"Who's your surgeon?" He asked as papers shuffled around on the other end of the line. "Wait, I found your paperwork. You're on clear fluids tomorrow and bowel prep starting on Wednesday. Fitting in two COVID tests as well won't be easy. I can contact—"

"Wait, what?" I cut in, completely blindsided by his casual mention of the restrictions I was supposed to be following.

"The instructions from your surgeon are for you to fast for two days on liquids. The first day is liquid, then on the second day—the day prior to surgery—you are to be on clear fluids only. On Wednesday, you are also instructed to do a 'full bowel cleanse to ensure all material has been evacuated from the large intestine,'" he said, obviously reading the directive verbatim from the forms in front of him.

"You're looking at the instructions for me right now? For Ashleigh Matthews?" I asked, convinced he had the wrong paperwork in hand.

"Yes," he replied, then paused.

"This is literally the first time I've heard that I need to do any of that this week." I wasn't sure I had enough liquids of any colour or consistency in the house for me to survive on for two days, and I definitely didn't have the medication needed to do a full evacuation of my bowel. "You're saying I'm supposed to be on a liquid diet for two days literally beginning tomorrow?" I was stunned both by the instructions and also the method by which I had discovered their existence.

"I think the best way forward here is for me to ask the anesthesiologist to call you for pre-admission. She may determine that you're unable to be sedated regardless of a negative swab, and then we won't need to co-ordinate multiple tests," he suggested.

Or consider what to do about my total lack of preparation for two days of fasting.

Less than half an hour later, I'd concluded the discussion with the anesthesiologist in which she determined that regardless of my swab results, I was too congested to safely be put under general anesthesia and, therefore, my surgery would have to be postponed. This was perhaps best on several fronts, as postponement gave me time to pick up the medications I would need for bowel preparation, as well as a variety of fluids on which to sustain myself while fasting. The difference between a liquid diet and a clear-fluids-only diet can best be explained by comparing smoothies and pureed soups to bone broth and ginger ale, and I needed time to be sure to have an ample stock of both.

Oophorectomy Round Two was booked for two weeks after my initial surgery date, giving me plenty of time to recover from the head cold prior to being sedated for surgery. I was also scheduled to have the required molecular COVID-19 swab the afternoon of my second oophorectomy pre-admission appointment, and the result of that testing confirmed my readiness for surgery. I began the liquid diet the next day and then the clear-fluid-only diet the day after that. I also took the first of two doses of a powdered evil mixed with water that caused the entire contents of my small and large intestines to rush from my body over the course of the twenty-four hours after each dose. This second day of restricted nutrition was especially tortuous because I could no longer have even the protein shakes that had quelled my feelings of hunger the day before. Add in the forceful evacuation that the powdered evil signalled to my colon and it was just an awful, awful day in every way.

As the surgery finish line drew closer and closer, I was hanging on for dear life to get the operation over with so I could eat solid food and stop pooping. On the eve of surgery, I was so overwhelmed with hunger and discomfort that I made my family eat their supper down in the basement while I sat in bed upstairs sobbing. I couldn't bear the possibility of smelling their luxurious meal if they ate it at the kitchen table down the hall from my bed.

At 7:30 p.m. on the evening before my bilateral salpingo-oophorectomy, I was lying in bed with Bean, helping her get to sleep. I had taken my second dose of powdered evil a few hours prior and was planning on staying in bed with her until I had to get up the next morning because I was so weak from lack of food and angry from lack of food and sad from lack of food. Bean was not yet asleep, and I was listening to a podcast on my headphones with my notifications turned off as we cuddled. Just as I could feel Bean's breathing beginning to deepen, the screen on my phone lit up from its position on the bedside table as it silently indicated an incoming call. I could see the screen from where I was laying without needing to move my body, and I could identify that it was a private number calling. Initially, I assumed that it was a scam phone call, so I didn't answer it as my sudden voice in the quiet room would have disturbed an almost-asleep kid—something no parent does for any reason outside of a legitimate emergency. Seconds later, a voicemail message popped up on the screen and my heart raced. Scammers don't often leave a callback number, and I suddenly realized who else might be calling so late on the eve of a medical procedure.

While still lying in bed with Bean, I checked my voicemail and heard the frantic voice of my surgeon's receptionist in my headphones telling me that my surgeon had developed two symptoms of COVID-19 and was required to self-isolate until he had a test that returned a negative result—something that could not happen for at least forty-eight hours. My surgery for the following morning—less than twelve hours away at that point—had to be cancelled. The receptionist was so kind, so unnecessarily apologetic, and desperate to reach me before the following morning when I would otherwise have shown up at the hospital ready to go, with no surgeon present.

I do not remember getting out of the bed and walking down the hall to the couch where Ava and Scott sat. I do not remember putting my phone on speaker and replaying the message. But I do remember Scott's face of despair and anguish when he understood what the receptionist was telling us and him exclaiming, "No!"

Obviously this was not some elaborate joke, obviously my surgeon did not cancel scheduled procedures lightly, and doing so was the only action possible in a COVID-19 world; however, it was not until hearing Scott's anguish that my mind and my body absorbed the reality of the situation and the floodgates of my emotions broke.

I lay my head in his lap on the couch and I wept harder than I had at perhaps any point along my treatment path until then. My tears were a result of the postponed surgery, but the postponement of my surgery was also the final gram of emotional weight I could hold before the dam broke and everything I had been holding back for the past year spilled out. Scott began to explain to Ava what was going on and why my surgery was suddenly not happening in the morning, and she interrupted him.

"Go make Mom some food! Now!" she yelled.

She asked me what I wanted and ran to the kitchen herself, an eight year old fully prepared to conjure anything I asked for. If I had told my daughter that I desired filet mignon at that moment, she would have tried her absolute best to make that happen. Between wracking sobs, I tried to focus on what I most wanted to put into my depleted and desolate stomach, and the first thing that came to my mind was popcorn.

Before I'd even finished the statement "popcorn, I want popcorn," I could hear Scott and Ava pulling the popcorn popper from the cupboard and the kernels from the pantry. I managed to calm myself enough to join them in the kitchen, but then as the popcorn began to pop and the smell wafted to my nose, I lost all composure and sank to the kitchen floor to weep again over the impossible situation COVID-19 had put us all in. The knowledge that I would have to do the pre-surgery prep all over again from the beginning before my salpingo-oophorectomy was complete brought me literally to my knees.

That popcorn was the best fucking food I'd ever tasted in my life.

CHAPTER FORTY-FIVE

After a digestive system has been fasting for two days, it takes another day or so for the stomach and bowels to readjust to their previous capabilities. It was the weekend—three days after the shattering phone call—before I felt fully back to normal as far as my physical strength and my digestive confidence could be assessed. Thankfully, the surgeon was free of COVID-19 and could rebook me as early as the week after, but I simply did not have the ability to repeat the pre-surgical requirements so soon. Additionally, during the emotional and gastrointestinal recovery of the days after my second attempt at having my ovaries removed, I'd reached the conclusion that the surgeon I had been referred to was not the right fit for my needs during cancer care. In no way was this conclusion a result of the cancellation of my second surgery attempt, as postponing was the only responsible and honest course of action that could have been taken in the context of a pandemic. I had legitimate reasons for considering changing medical professionals that I will not delineate here; however, my reasons were personal and not due to any breach of ethics or medicine. This distinction between malpractice and preference made the realization that I did not align with this surgeon slower to formulate within my own mind, and more difficult to articulate even once it was identified.

Asking for a new doctor is not easy, but it was a privilege I had because I live in a place with multiple gynecological surgeons who could perform the surgery I needed. The discussions Scott and I had regarding changing surgeons invariably ended with me accepting that if I did choose to switch to another surgeon, my surgery would be delayed, possibly for a few months. Referral to a new doctor at that point would begin the process of getting on the operating table over from the beginning, whereas the surgeon I had already met with could fit me into his operating schedule within a week. In the end, I decided that I needed to listen to my instincts and choose a different surgeon to perform this procedure. One week after my second surgery postponement, I spoke to the office of the gynecological surgeon and told them that I would be pursuing my procedure with another clinic.

It would be another two months before I met with the gynecological surgeon who would remove my ovaries.

CHAPTER FORTY-SIX

The very first consultation with my new surgeon happened during the lowest level of pandemic restrictions that Newfoundland would be under all year, and I was able to meet with him in person at his office. Our discussion of the procedure was initially very similar to my discussion with the previous surgeon because I began once again by sharing the results of my CHEK2 genetic mutation findings.

"I would like to have both ovaries and also fallopian tubes removed in this surgery."

"I understand why you'd want that. This procedure includes the removal of the portion of the fallopian tubes that the ovaries are housed within, as this is the likely first place that cancer would present."

Checked my first major talking point off the list.

"Let's discuss expectations after the procedure," he carried on. "The surgery is completed laparoscopically, which means only small incisions are made on your abdomen and a camera is inserted through the incisions made. There will be three incisions in total, sometimes four but not often."

"How large are the incisions?" I asked.

"Perhaps a stitch or two will be needed for each one afterwards, so quite small. Nothing like the scar lines I am sure you have from your chest surgeries."

"Oh! Okay. That sounds like it will be much easier to recover from as well," I replied.

"As far as wound care goes, yes. From the perspective of overall recovery, you will still need to take it easy after discharge. You cannot lift anything over five pounds for four weeks to ensure proper healing of the incisions I will make inside your body during the removal of your ovaries. You will also have an appointment with a community health nurse to have your sutures removed about ten days after the surgery."

"My face is well known around community health."

The surgeon smiled and carried on discussing the procedure in more detail.

"You should expect bleeding similar to a moderate menstrual period for a few days afterwards. You'll need to keep period products of whatever variety you prefer on hand, just no tampons or menstrual cups for four weeks after surgery—nothing that is inserted."

"That makes sense, but I hadn't considered it at all," I replied and made a note to pick up a stock of pads.

He referred to the intake forms I'd filled out in the waiting room and moved on to the next topic. "Your menopause symptoms include hot flushes now, I see. Are they significant?"

"I would call them significant, yes," I confirmed. "They happen multiple times every day, and some of them can be vicious."

"The removal of your ovaries may impact the hot flushes, too. They may lesson in severity, quantity, or perhaps even both once you are permanently menopausal. They may worsen slightly at first, but most patients that have gone through surgical menopause have reported that they do drop off quickly not long afterwards."

"I'd be going ahead with this surgery even if the procedure

wouldn't impact the hot flushes, but I am happy to hear that there is potential that they'll be lessened. I had no idea that being fully menopausal could impact the situation positively."

"There's hope!" he responded. "Speaking of motivation for the surgery, have you discussed pathology after the surgery with anyone?" he asked.

"No. I assume I'll get a report eventually?"

"You're undergoing this surgery as prevention for cancer and not eradication; however, your ovaries and fallopian tubes will still be examined by a pathologist after they are removed." I pictured the pathology meat slicer once again, this time with my ovaries being sliced wafer thin by the blade.

"And if there is cancer there already?" I asked. "I'm here to prevent that outcome, but what if cancer has beaten me to the scalpel and it's already there?"

"Ultimately, it would be a discussion to have with your medical oncologist as well, but in that scenario a radical hysterectomy is the likely next step," he replied, confirming what I assumed.

"That does happen, does it? A patient comes in to prevent cancer and finds out that it's too late?" I was preparing for that eventuality already, even if just at the edges of my mind.

"Yes, cancer can be found to be present in that situation," he confirmed, another medical professional telling me the whole truth. "I wouldn't consider it to be too late, though. If cancer cells are discovered, they'd have been found and removed before they even caused symptoms. Assuming that cancer found in your ovaries is a second primary cancer and not metastatic breast cancer, which would be highly unusual, I would consider that finding exceedingly early and not too late."

"Right. I guess if it's there, it's there. Might as well know now." I felt resigned to a life that would always consider the presence of cancer, and I could hear that resignation in my voice.

"I agree," he said, before moving on to discuss scheduling the surgery. "Now, as far as my operative calendar goes, we are looking at early in the new year."

The timeline with this surgeon would see me back in the operating room in a little over a month and a half, a fact that I easily accepted as I could now enjoy the holiday season with my family without once again being in recovery from surgery.

Over the next six weeks, my family and I celebrated Christmas and New Year's together with the same modifications that so many families had to add to their traditions to celebrate safely in a pandemic world. We did not see as many friends as we normally would have and we limited our contacts to grandparents and very close friends. This was also the first major family celebration since my diagnosis of cancer that was coupled with the knowledge that I would likely survive.

CHAPTER FORTY-SEVEN

I got the call in early January that my oophorectomy was scheduled for January 15th, 2021. I was ready to take this next bite, whether it brought with it a discovery of more cancer cells or it gave me peace of mind that estrogen would no longer play a major role in future cancer growth—or both. This surgeon did not require bowel prep prior to surgery; therefore, the three days leading up to the surgery were full of pre-admission appointments, another molecular COVID-19 swab followed by isolation, and then fasting only during the evening before surgery. I packed a bag for a two-night hospital stay even though I was expected to go home the same afternoon, and Scott and I joked that if there was any snow forecasted—and I mean *any*—that we'd stay home. This was, after all, not only my first surgery after Snowmageddon, but also just two days shy of the first anniversary of the storm itself.

Surgery day arrived with no snow—no obstacles in front of me at all—and before I knew it, I was smelling the antiseptic air of an operating room once again. This time, I had extra arm bands on my body alerting staff not to administer any IVs, take any blood, or perform blood pressure checks on my right arm due to my lack of axillary lymph nodes, but otherwise everything was achingly familiar.

Yet again, I put on two gowns, one opening in front and one in the back, I packed my clothing into the plastic bag for patient personal effects, and I handed over my glasses just as I had done three times before. I closed my eyes on the operating table for the fourth time, and I was still not prepared for the emotional and physiological disconnect of waking up one second later after an hour had passed. This time, I had not a moment of belief that I might make it through without being ill. I could feel it as soon as I was able to keep my eyes open long enough to discern where I was.

Not only did COVID-19 safety protocols make it impossible for Scott to be at my side as I was recovering from anesthesia this time, he wasn't even allowed to wait for me anywhere inside the hospital. After I had been prepared for surgery and left the pre-op area to walk to the operating room, he left the hospital and went home to await a call from the nursing staff telling him I was awake and ready for him to return and pick me up.

The nurse in the recovery area helped me move my legs and body in order to get my circulation moving and push the sedatives through my body, but I was moving my body parts against the waves of a nausea tsunami once again, and it was only a matter of time before it crashed against my insides. I was still sporting two hospital gowns when the tsunami finally arrived, but I'd had time to put on my underwear before I was once again on all fours on a hospital gurney heaving again and again, trying to force up the nothing that was inside my stomach.

The force of my nausea was just as remarkable as all previous occasions, and I was immediately afraid that it would cause another bleeding issue. Once the first wave of heaving diminished, I became deeply grateful that my surgeon had alerted me to the likelihood of vaginal bleeding after surgery because his warning was the only reason I had arrived that morning with cloth pads in my hospital bag. Because of the bodily location of this surgery, the repercussions of my internal tsunami were felt at every exit, and no other medical professional had even alluded to the possibility of bleeding, nor offered me any sanitary products post-op. Had I not been told to expect this bleeding by my surgeon, I would have been wholly and drastically unprepared.

After a second dose of vomiting—this time less intensely violent than the first—I managed to clean myself up, finish getting dressed, and then make my way into the wheelchair at my bedside so I could make my hospital exit. After all of the ridiculous scenarios complicating my previous operations, I believed that being admitted after this procedure was a more likely outcome than being discharged, so it was with mild disbelief that I found myself being wheeled out of the elevator and through the exit into the waiting arms of my husband. I could not believe that it was finally, finally done. I was fully and irrevocably menopausal, and with just one more pathology report remaining, I might also be done with surgeries necessitated by cancer.

We drove home and all along the way I knew there was at least one more epic wave of violent sickness within me. My oldest daughter has a deep fear of anything related to vomiting and I knew she would not wish to witness the ferocity with which I was sick after anesthesia. Somehow, I managed to get inside the house and tell her to vacate before I was ill for another time. Once again, I was on all fours and violently sick; however, this time I was on my own floor and with Scott kneeling beside my convulsing body as I heaved and heaved. As this bout of gastrointestinal violence crested and passed, I knew I was done with it. Scott got me upstairs and into bed, and I slept for the remainder of that day and the night that followed. When I woke the next morning I was sore, but I was back in recovery mode, and recovery mode is also a subject I have a master's degree in.

I had significantly less trauma internally and externally than when I awoke after my mastectomy or my axillary lymph node surgery because of the less invasive laparoscopic method of the salpingo-oophorectomy. A little over a week later, I was due to have the stitches removed from the three small incisions I carried, three sutures in my belly button and two each in two spots on my left side above my hip. The forecast worsened and worsened all week leading up to the appointment, and forty-eight hours beforehand, a winter storm warning was issued for the very day that I was to go and have the itchy, irritating stitches removed. Scott was off on leave from work since I was prohibited from lifting anything, and once the winter storm warning was issued, there was nothing left to do but laugh at my unimaginable appointment luck.

"I think we should stay home. Why tempt fate?" I said to him.

"I think staying home in a January snowstorm is a good idea," he initially agreed. "Except those stitches are making you miserably uncomfortable."

"They are," I confirmed. I knew I had been insufferable in my complaints about their itchiness. "That's why I think you should take the stitches out and we can avoid leaving the house in a snowstorm."

"You want me to remove your stitches?" he asked, without even the decency to pretend to be surprised that I would suggest he do such a thing. We were well past the threshold of amateur suture removal in our relationship by then.

"I do. And, I want you to remove them right now," I stated. "If you're going to do it to avoid travelling in a blizzard two days from now, why wait? The incisions are clearly healed," I concluded.

This is how my husband added suture removal to his repertoire of skills, and I would recommend him to anyone considering home removal after abdominal surgery in an effort to avoid driving in a winter storm. I barely felt a thing.

CHAPTER FORTY-EIGHT

One month after my ovaries and fallopian tubes were removed, I had a telephone appointment with my gynecological oncology surgeon to receive the pathology report on the condition of my excised reproductive organs. By this time, a COVID-19 variant outbreak had occurred and the entire province was in a lockdown again, so I could only receive this information via telephone. My doctor told me that everything in the pathology report reflected how utterly normal the surgery had gone and how utterly normal my ovaries appeared to be under a microscope. I asked my doctor for a copy of the report and he emailed it to me immediately for my own reading.

This pathology report was all celebrating, no consolation. Nothing needed to be monitored, mitigated, or removed. While reading the description of a segment of one of my fallopian tubes, I saw it: after mentioning a small paratubal cyst, something exceedingly common and not at all concerning, the pathologist had described my fallopian tube as "otherwise grossly unremarkable".

Goddammit, what a beautiful phrase. Never in my life have I ever been so fucking happy to be,

otherwise grossly unremarkable.

EPILOGUE

Recovery Is Not Linear

In the early summer of the year after my mastectomy and lymph node removal, I was hiking with my kids in a forested park. It was one of the first times we'd been outside for an extended period of time since my surgeries and we'd planned for a few hours in the sunshine and amongst the trees. I had my backpack full of snacks and we had a wonderful morning. It wasn't until we returned home and I took off the cross-body bag that I'd used that day that I realized I had a large blister emerging across my chest. I was less than a year past my bilateral mastectomy and I had no feeling across the scar line on my chest or for several centimetres above and below the battle line across my upper body. The front buckle of my backpack had been rubbing on my scar line as it bisected my chest and I hadn't realized because it was happening in the dead zone. It was obvious that I couldn't wear that backpack anymore and that I would need a two-shoulder companion from then on.

I'd been sewing as a hobby for years; however, that hobby became necessity after my chest surgery. My breastless silhouette eliminated just about every top with a feminine cut as well as every fitted dress available off the rack. Moving from clothing into experimentation with making a backpack didn't seem daunting to me as a self-assessed "adventurous beginner" sewist. I swiftly settled on a backpack in a rucksack style and while I cursed more than once as I tried to get that damned zipper to fit in and be functional, I completed the project relatively quickly and loved the result. In the year after I completed it, I received countless compliments while I waited for appointments at the Cancer Centre, on trips to the library with my kids, and especially while exploring the outdoors with my family. This is how a kernel of an idea began to take root, suggesting to me that I might be able to create a business making that rucksack for others. It took a long time for me to convince myself that I had the skills, both as a sewist to complete the physical work and also as a human who would need to market my rucksacks, but when I finally leapt it was into a business making backpacks that I called Ramble.

I began selling my handmade rucksacks at farmers' markets and craft fairs in my local community in the early months after I'd begun my business. Since that beginning, I have met so many incredible artists and artisans while attending local events. I see their prints displayed on my walls, their tees on my husband, and their knitted hats on my kids' heads; I have enjoyed handmade donuts, spectacular jams, and more than one sandwich that I salivate just thinking about now. The people I have connected with as event organizers and artists and the people I have connected with as my customers are often among the most genuine and giving I have ever known, and I would not have met any of them had it not been for my need for a bag that didn't blister my fragile chest. I would not have met any of them were it not for my breast cancer. Reconciling the fact that a disease that nearly took my life also played a pivotal part in opening a life of accomplishment and validation through textile art—and through writing—is an aspect of survivorship that is as chronic as the disease itself. I will never be grateful for the cancer that I had and I will never be grateful that this disease exists and persists because it has taken so much and so many from me and from people that I care about. The despair that I feel when I look in the mirror some days is real and will never go away—but so is the joy I feel when I see those artisan friends setting up beside and around me at a market.

I expect that I will forever be seeking the balance between gratitude for the things cancer illuminated in its wake and grief for the things cancer has stolen because the weight of the items on both sides of that scale are forever in flux. All I can do is respect their present weight and hope that sharing my experience adds a little to the right side.

SUPPLEMENTARY

Words Especially for Those Who Come Behind Me

Most people think they know how they'd react to a cancer diagnosis and I'm willing to bet most are totally wrong. We all experience some combination of tears, panic, angry screaming, and numbness in the hours or days after being told cancer has been found, but that's not what I am referring to. No one will predict which small and inconsequential incident will be the final straw that destroys the person newly dealing with the reality of cancer until it happens. No one truly knows what they'd write on the paper to leave behind for their kids or their partner until they're hours away from major surgery and have to put the pencil to the paper and write it.

There are aspects of every type of cancer that are uniquely awful because of the placement, treatment, necessary surgery, or maintenance needed to best approach the type and stage diagnosed. I can only speak from the position of a woman who has battled a stage 3 diagnosis of breast cancer. I do not speak for every cancer patient, but I can speak for me and I can speak about the common struggles that I hear so many of my fellow cancer patient friends dealing with. These final pages are written especially for the people who have crossed the ocean from cellular normie to cellular deviant with any type of cancer and that are now understanding just how much they did not understand of life after facing their own mortality.

Welcome to the terrible, terrible club of Cancer Patient.

Expect Overwhelm:

If you feel yourself going cross-eyed at the medical jargon and pharmacological names that are swirling around you in doctors' offices, give yourself permission to check out. Ask someone to take notes for you, and then trust the knowledge and professionalism of the oncologists and Cancer Centre staff around you when the overwhelm becomes too great. The difficulty of being a Cancer Muggle with cancer, especially when surrounded by highly educated medical professionals who wish to contribute to saving your life, is that your deficit in understanding is magnified by the emotional toll you are also attempting to carry. It is not just that you do not understand the language being spoken at appointments, it's that you do not understand the language *and* you are terrified of dying. As I sat on the floor of my general practitioner's exam room listening to him describe ductal carcinoma in situ, I was a Cancer Muggle with cancer. If you are there now, or were not so long ago, know that we all began in that same awful place on the floor.

Accept Compassion:

My second diagnostic appointment, the one in which the radiologist personally walked me to the mammogram machine, was the first time I experienced the absolutely incredible compassion that the majority of the professionals working in cancer care offer to patients. I have had radiation therapists invite my husband and kids into the radiation therapy room to see the machine that I would be laying in and patiently answer all their questions. My lymphedema nurse kept my youngest company while I went to the bathroom so Bean wouldn't have to hang out in the stall with me. A porter regularly brought Popsicles to my kids whenever they accompanied me to appointments.

I suspect that this kindness, patience, and fearlessness in the face of grief and sorrow is present not because these specific people are exemplary in their field but rather that the medical professionals who are drawn to build a career in cancer care are the most compassionate individuals among humanity. The Cancer Centre in every community is filled to the rafters with porters that know where the Popsicles are and nurses who will bring you a cup of tea while you sit and receive chemotherapy because those are the exact types of people who wish to be in those positions within their communities. Accept the compassion and know that they expect nothing in return.

Face Mortality:

It doesn't matter what stage your cancer is, you are allowed to be crushed and scared and determined and everything else that you feel as you move through diagnosis, treatment, and survivorship. If Ashleigh of now could go back and sit beside Ashleigh of the early days in my diagnosis, I would spend a significant amount of time telling myself that cancer is cancer. While some cancers are inherently more life threatening than others, while some cancers necessitate treatment processes that are especially horrifying, while some cancers respond more reliably to the most horrendous chemotherapy regimens and some to the least, they are all still cancers.

Every single person that sits across from a trusted medical professional to be told that they have any type of cancer faces their own mortality in the same way. There is no curve for how shitty it is to believe you could die, it's just terrible for everyone who faces it. Ultimately, I did not die. I have friends who have died and I have friends who are going to die. None of those who died would want me to blunt the edges of the grief I harbour for myself just because I happened to live, and I know this because those friends are exactly the people I have talked to about it.

To be clear, this is not a pass to centre personal grief and fear at all times. When at the funeral of a friend after the conclusion of their own cancer battle, don't tell all those in attendance about your struggles and eventual success with the same chemotherapy that their loved one was not successful with. That's just being an ass. It is, however, healthy and valid to shed tears for your own losses and struggles with your own supportive friends and family. Time and place matters, but it also matters that you don't invalidate your own grief by disallowing it to ever surface under the guise of "so many have it so much worse"-isms.

Seek Legacy:

I believe there is a legacy that I have inherited as a cancer patient. The advances in approach to cancer treatment and maintenance that I benefit from tremendously are due to the bravery and selflessness of cancer warriors before me who have donated their time, thoughts, blood, sweat, and tumours to the scientists and doctors who insist that we can fight this disease better. From the patients who volunteered to be experimented on with chemotherapy drugs, ultimately aiding in refining dosages and combinations that work, to those who underwent experimental surgical procedures with the hopes of learning about how and why cancer spreads the way it does, we would not be making strides against this physiological foe without people who are willing to put their very bodies forward for the purposes of advancing science.

In addition to participating in the genetic research of the RuBY study, I opted in for the main component of RuBY as well. Before I began receiving chemotherapy I provided blood samples to the study, and later, after my bilateral mastectomy, I donated all remaining portions of my carcinoma that could be useful to the study as well. I've spent hours answering surveys on my experiences through my cancer treatment and I have given the researchers access to my health records as they relate to my diagnosis and treatment.

To date, I have volunteered for nearly a dozen different studies that seek cancer patient participants or that strive to research the medical experiences I've had throughout my life as a cancer patient and thriver. The more I talk to researchers, the more I see and hear how grateful they are for any individual willing to volunteer for medical research and the more I realize how scarce participants for medical studies often are. Some initiatives asked for blood or saliva and I readily provided those. Other research projects ask for my time, a more precious commodity than my blood, and I readily give that as well. I owe so much to the patients who tried horrendous chemotherapy drugs and endured painful medical procedures that inched our understanding of medicine, cancer, and treatment efficacy forward. My gratitude for their sacrifice is paid forward with my own donations of tumour, time, and story.

Whenever any manageable opportunity is presented to me to perhaps make a small contribution to the advancement of understanding the mechanism of this bullshit disease, you better believe I will always be all-fucking-in. I acknowledge that there are barriers to volunteer participation in medical research and that participation isn't for everyone; however, if you find yourself in the position physically and emotionally to give, I don't think you will regret it.

Build Support:

The staff inside the walls of a Cancer Centre are compassionate without limit. The budgets that a Cancer Centre operates within, however, are not. There is a demographic mismatch between the under-forty patient and the services readily available within arms' reach at many Cancer Centres because most patients are in their sixties or older. When operating on a limited and insufficient budget, priorities for programming are given to the types of support that will help the majority of patients, and so it naturally follows that few Cancer Centres are designed with the needs and survivorship of young adults specifically in mind.

Child care is often a problem for young-adult cancer patients in a way that it simply isn't for those who have children old enough to drive them to appointments. Most, if not all, Cancer Centres have social work or counselling services available for those who request it; precious few have sexual health professionals or fertility specialists available to aid couples after cancer when it has affected sex drive, sexual ability, or fertility.

If you are a young adult who is experiencing a cancer diagnosis, building your own support network right now should be top of mind. Include emotional support like a psychiatrist or psychologist, as well as para-health professionals like a massage therapist, physiotherapist, or kinesiologist. Find a yoga studio, art studio, music class, swimming pool you like—whatever your thing is—and start to do it now, so you will be in a familiar place whenever you feel strong enough to incorporate movement and activity into your days between treatments. Lastly, connect with groups of other people sharing similar experiences as soon as you are able. Whether it's a group of other cancer patients of the same general age, who have the same type of cancer, who live in the same geographical area, or being with groups of people who have faced a similar diagnosis from a similar position as you, it will be invaluable when you encounter the missing pieces of support within your own Cancer Centre services.

Long Term:

For lots of people who undergo treatment for advanced stages of cancer, the side effects from treatment stay around for the long term. In the years after my diagnosis, one of my doctors listened to my description of recurring pain that I experience and told me that cancer is a chronic disease for me, not an acute one. That description continues to resonate with me today because, although

I do not presently have (known) cancer cells in my body, I deal with the after-effects of the eradication of the cancer cells that I did have every day.

My nails have never regained their pre-chemotherapy strength or composition and they break when under even the slightest force. Six months after I finished chemotherapy completely, I noticed that all my fingernails and toenails had alternating dark and light bands horizontally across them, like pale stripes. This was the evidence of Taxotere growing out from my nails and each band of lightness to darkness marked a three-week time span between treatments when the nails would begin to grow stronger—only to be blasted once again by chemotherapy's destructive forces.

The mouth sores that began during chemotherapy still pop up on my tongue in the exact same place once every two or three months—an indication that the echo of cytotoxic medication continues to reverberate inside my body.

Some days, the nerve pain in my right arm and feet is next level and nobody has ever been able to address the pain or its source adequately.

Side effects from treatments will be different for every cancer patient, but odds are that every patient will have lasting consequences—in addition to being alive. I was told time and time again that the likelihood of each side effect was minimal; however, I have also never been asked directly whether I experienced any of those specific side effects afterwards. If doctors are basing the "minimal likelihood" statement on reported patient experiences, they are falling short of actually asking patients what they experience, and we can't remember all the possible side effects to all the medications and interventions we undergo to report back on our specific suffering. Assume you will have long-term side effects of treatment like chemotherapy, radiation therapy, and surgery, and you can avoid the frustration of wondering why you are part of that "minimal likelihood" group that we are all actually a part of.

Carry Survivorship:

Guilt will creep in at times as we question why we are one of the ones who battled cancer and lived on after. There is no definable reason why Taxotere, Adriamycin, and cyclophosphamide stopped my carcinoma in its tracks, only for them to prove ineffective on the carcinoma of another hormone-responsive breast cancer patient. No one can point to a reason that my cancer sped into my lymph nodes but no farther before being detected, and yet other young patients with cancer know nothing until the cancer cells have already taken up home in the bones, the lungs, the brain. The question of why one person gets to live when another person who maintained the same determination and strength dies is unanswerable, and this is where survivor guilt is born. Try to allow yourself some grace when the guilt comes for you too, because we'll both know that the truth is we did nothing special to save ourselves. There is nothing about me as a human that makes me more or less remarkable than any other human battling cancer, and yet I am here, you are here too, and so many others are not. The unfairness of this fact can never truly be reconciled, so do what you can with the life you have in front of you without letting guilt hold you back.

ACKNOWLEDGEMENTS

To Breakwater Books for taking the chance on me and believing that I had something worthwhile to say, and to Christine Gordon-Manley for helping me refine those things so they made sense outside of my own head.

To Dr. Joy McCarthy, Dr. Terri Stuckless, Dr. Alex Mathieson, and Dr. Trent Parsons and all of their clinic staff—many of whom have literally or figuratively held my hand at some point. Also, Michelle Burke for showing me how to cultivate the tools needed to withstand the emotional toil of a cancer diagnosis.

To the chemotherapy unit nursing staff, the Cancer Centre staff, and the community health nursing staff, I appreciate you and see all the things you do for the people who move through your offices and waiting rooms.

To Wanda and Ron Matthews, Ron Matthews and Christine Rainey, Ray and Chris Miller; and Meaghan Burridge, Meghan Careen, Crystal Chafe, Amy Muirhead, Lacey Pike, Rebecca Priestley-Harvey, Becca Robertson, and all their partners—I know you'd all do anything for me as I fought.

To Ashleigh, for reaching back to take my hand on this cancer road, even after you knew your burden was heavy; and to Michael for allowing me to talk about the friendship she and I shared.

To Karen's parents, Wayne and Maxine Jones, and her sisters, Tracey Young and Amanda Bruce, thank you for allowing me to share a small amount of the impact Karen had on my life. I know I am not the only one.

To Ava and Bean who, with their mere existence, provided me with the motivation to record my cancer experience as it happened, just in case I wasn't around to share it later. As it turns out, I am, but you still have to read this book when you're older anyway.

And finally, to Scott. What else can I say about your support and companionship? I suppose I can quote Cleopatra and say, "Fool! Don't you see now that I could have poisoned you a hundred times had I been able to live without you." But seriously though, if you do outlive me, please return my library books after I'm gone—I'm sure there will be plenty around no matter when I go.

ASHLEIGH MATTHEWS holds a BA in Cultural Anthropology from Memorial University of Newfoundland and Labrador. She is also a textile artist and sewist. In addition to sharing her experiences with breast cancer, she cares deeply about her homeschooling community, the artist and maker communities around her, as well as the many friends she has met who share the experience of a cancer diagnosis. She lives with her best friend and their two kids in a home centered directly between the Atlantic Ocean and their own forest in Conception Bay South, Newfoundland and Labrador.